THE TIPTOEING VALKYRIE

The Life of Test Pilot
VAN H. SHEPARD

2018

Van Shepard with his "Hoverbuggy", ca 1965

THE TIPTOEING VALKYRIE

The Life of Test Pilot
VAN H. SHEPARD

BILL SHEPARD, JR.

First printing: 2018

Manufacturing by CreateSpace, an Amazon company

ISBN-13: 978-1985897748 (paperback)
ISBN-10: 1985897741 (paperback)

Published by:
Bill Shepard, Jr.
1942 Buckthorn Court
Troy, MI 48098

For Addison and Brendan

Contents

Foreword   9

PART I: *Taking Off*   13

One   Firstborn   17

Two   This Kid Likes Airplanes!   23

Three   Hangin' at Selman   29

Four   "You're in the Army (Air Forces) Now"   39

Five   Wings!   47

PART II: *Test Pilot*   59

Six   Muroc   63

Seven   Okinawa   75

Eight   AFIT   89

Nine   Test Pilot School   97

Ten   Mach 1!   103

Eleven   On to North American   113

PART III: *"Ride of the Valkyries"*   121

Twelve   Betty   125

Thirteen   Mach 2!   131

Fourteen   Valkyrie   141

Fifteen   Maiden Flight   149

Sixteen   Double Shifts   157

PART IV: *Destiny*   165

    Seventeen   Mach 3!   171

    Eighteen   TIFS   179

    Nineteen   Guppies   187

    Twenty   The Twin-Trunk Pine   193

Epilogue   197

Appendices

    A: Milestones of Van Shepard's Aviation Career   203

    B: Van Shepard Family Tree   205

    C: Aircraft Flown Professionally by Van Shepard   207

Acknowledgments   209

Index   213

Foreword

This work is a biography of the life of my uncle Van H. Shepard. It is non-fictional. Or shall I say, it is based on an extensive compilation of factual memorabilia on Van, but it does have some blanks here and there filled in with educated guesses by me. For the latter, I have interpolated among recollections of relatives, inferences taken from the literature, and reference material on persons and events associated with Van's own life experiences. With regard to the four-part account of XB-70A flight 1-37, I acknowledge that the conversation dialogue and some of the specifics in Van's landing are according to my imagination.

The majority of these "factual memorabilia" is a wonderful collection of forty-two letters written between 1943 and 1968, all in Van's own hand, to his family in Louisiana. Most are from his years in the United States Air Force; all are quite detailed, even sheathed in their original envelopes, whose return addresses and postmarks aided historical characterization. There are also two other letters written by his wife Betty, equally detailed. The book features many excerpts taken verbatim from these letters.

Having the letters has been especially important in Van's case: not available to me was his military record on twelve-plus years of active duty, normally accessible from the National Personnel Records Center in St. Louis, Missouri. There was a disastrous fire there in 1973 which destroyed the records of all Air Force personnel with surnames beginning with I through Z, who were discharged from 1947 through 1964. It almost seemed there was a conspiracy against the re-creation of Van Shepard's career.

I have also used countless photographs obtained from family members and others. Most, of course, are of Van, from his infancy to within a few weeks of his death. Many show him with his aircraft, some of which have visible serial numbers aiding determination of site and date. But I also have several photographs taken by Van himself, mostly of those two things dearest to him: the women in his life and the aircraft in his life. To be honest, I am not sure in which order those two passions should be listed.

In addition to the letters and photographs, I have used many other memorabilia such as certificates of achievement, a cockpit voice recording, air incident reports by Van, a collection of his workplace badges, a state government commendation, and even travel expense reports. I have also used several books and media articles on the many aircraft types that Van flew. All of these sources have been critical to my ability to create his life's story.

Of course, I also have leveraged family members. The Shepard family has been blessed with impressive longevity: except for one sister who died as a toddler, all of Van's siblings survive as of this publishing. I have interviewed all of them and their spouses. I also was fortunate to communicate with one of Van's girlfriends from his Air Force days.

Last but not least, I have my own extensive recollections of my uncle. Of his fourteen nephews and nieces, I am the eldest, the only one to have reached adulthood as of his passing. Further, I was fortunate to have lived near him as a child in southern California, when he began his career as an industry test pilot. It is fair to say that Uncle Van has always been one of my heroes.

My motivation for writing this book? It's simple. Van Shepard accomplished a great deal in his field, contributing to the advancement of aviation, both in ensuring America's military air superiority, and in furthering the utility of commercial transport. He gave his life in the pursuit of the latter. But he had no children of his own. There has been no one to tell his story in the more than forty-seven years since his death. I felt like it was up to me to start the process of ensuring my uncle's legacy.

Van Shepard's name is on one of the aircraft he flew in the National Museum of the United States Air Force near Dayton, Ohio. The mission of this book is to ensure that museum visitors seeing that name might have a way of finding out who this man was, and what he did for us all with his life.

Bill Shepard, Jr.
Troy, Michigan
September 2017

PART I

Taking Off

Caineville, Utah, 7 March 1966, 9:44 am MST

That little yellow light wasn't going away.

Joe Cotton thought to himself, "Man, not again."

It had been on for a few seconds now, and he watched as the needle on the #2 utility hydraulic system pressure gauge began to drop off. It wasn't two months earlier that he had the same problem, while sitting in the left seat of this very aircraft. This time it was worse, for two reasons: first, as copilot now, he was the one responsible for hydraulic systems, and, second, like any confident test pilot, he'd rather be flying the plane in an emergency, even though he trusted his pilot with his life.

Van Shepard's focus had been riveted on his descent from maximum altitude, paying no attention to the multi-colored rock formations of Capitol Reef far below, brilliantly illuminated by the morning sun. Pilots of research aircraft have always prided themselves in their performance to altitude schedule; it is one of the discriminators between the mere "competent" and the true "expert". And Shepard, North American Aviation XB-70 program engineering test pilot, would always consider himself in the latter cadre. Joining NAA following his US Air Force retirement in 1955, he had been rewarded with assignments of ever-increasing responsibility, and the risk that goes along with them.

Moreover, maintaining an altitude track was an even greater challenge in the Big White Bird: with its innovative compression lift design, the XB-70A Valkyrie demanded even more focused attention to instrumentation, and a deft hand on the yoke and throttles, to keep it on schedule.

Shepard had not noticed the light when his copilot tersely announced, "We're starting to lose U2."

Immediately his focus shifted to the U2 gauge. While he had seen hydraulic leaks in many prior flights, he had not experienced a total system loss. This was not good.

For its 37th flight, XB-70A Air Vehicle #1, serial no. 62-0001, had lifted its gleaming white half-million pounds off Edwards Air Force Base Runway 22 at 230 miles per hour, on the morning of Monday, 7 March 1966. The weather was excellent, as it had been for weeks now, after a wetter than normal early winter. On the agenda for this largest supersonic aircraft in US history was attainment of Mach 2.2, about 1,450 miles per hour, at 55,000 feet altitude. At various points in the flight schedule, the pilots were to perform tests on the Air Induction Control System (the variable geometry air inlets for the six jet engines), to record yaw, pitch, and roll responses to various control inputs, and to cycle throttle inputs to the engines, both individually and in combination. It was an ambitious agenda that would keep pilot and copilot fully occupied during the two hour flight, to which they were accustomed.

Colonel Joe Cotton, US Air Force XB-70 program project pilot, continued his appraisal of U2 hydraulic pressure with understatement. "It's dropping steadily."

Shepard could see this for himself.

Cotton called out, "Data Control, we've got a steady yellow on U2; came on at about four-one-one-zero. Pressure is at eighteen hundred and dropping fast."

"Four-one-one-zero" was the flight time stamp, indicating 4,110 seconds after takeoff, or a little over an hour into Flight 1-37.

The pilots heard the simple reply, "Roger that, One" in their headsets. They knew it would take a few seconds for the ground team and chase pilots to digest this sobering news.

Shepard thought to himself with disgust, "Bound to be. This has just gone too well up to now." He and Cotton were on their way to checking every box on their test card without incident. Among their successes was a near-perfect climb, the best Shepard had yet executed: right on plan all the way to 55,000 plus. Further, at Mach 2.2, it was the fastest of his eight XB-70 rides this year; it felt good. Oh well, at least they still had good pressure in the U1 (primary utility) hydraulics.

Seconds later, the unthinkable. The U1 light, this one monitoring the primary utility hydraulic pressure, illuminated. This time both pilots saw it, accompanied by the sickening counterclockwise movement in the U1 gauge's indicator.

Shepard let out a single emphatic "Damn."

Cotton barked into his mic, "Data Control, we've got U1 dropping now, repeat, U1 dropping at four-one-four-five, down to twenty-seven hundred."

After more time elapsed than with their reply to the U2 news, the Edwards Data Control room matter-of-factly came back, "Uh, roger, Zero-Zero-One, acknowledging lights in U1 and U2."

Those ground communicators would always try to sound even more nonchalant during emergencies, hoping to help their pilots maintain as much calm as possible.

This time Al White's voice crackled in the AV #1 headsets.

"Gotcha, One, roger U1 and U2; we're on our way, going AB now. Be there in a few minutes."

Secretly, White, chief test pilot at NAA's Los Angeles Division, wished it were him, but likewise had full confidence in the ability of his protege Van Shepard. White was in the TB-58A Hustler chase plane, which had been left behind twenty minutes earlier as the faster Valkyrie accelerated past Mach 2. In order to assist their stricken companions, the Hustler would go to afterburner ("AB") to rendezvous with AV #1 as soon as possible. In the meantime, Shepard pulled the six throttles back so that the Valkyrie, still traveling at over eleven hundred miles per hour, would begin to decelerate more quickly . . .

*   *   *

ONE

Firstborn

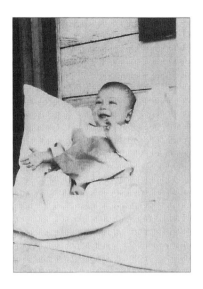

Van Shepard, 4 months

I T WAS SATURDAY, THE 4th of October, 1924, a warm northeast Louisiana day. The gas field workers had been spoiled by
the first fall-like weather of the season earlier in the week. Huber
Frederick Shepard had been working this field for five years, hired
into the Crescent Drilling Company by his foreman John Duchkar,
who was also the husband of his older sister Ruth. The Monroe field,
which would become the highest producing natural gas field on
earth, had already become the largest employer in the area. Huber
had made good money, tucking much of it away as savings, befitting

his thrifty nature.

Duchkar had come looking for him, finding him in a newly opened trench, dug to get at a leak in this line, a collector main crucial to the efficiency of the Ouachita Oil & Natural Gas Company's extensive works in the Monroe field. All he could see were shovelfuls of reddish-brown Louisiana earth flying out of the trench. Good ol' Hubie: Duchkar knew he could count on his brother-in-law to do whatever it took to isolate and repair the leak.

Marie & Huber, ca 1923

Huber was already hoping the crew could knock off early. He wanted to spend the rest of the short weekend at home with his bride of almost seventeen months, Frances Marie Van Dusen Shepard, now great with child, as they say. But he was nonetheless not quite ready for what he was to hear from John. His boss purposely informed him that his wife had gone into labor.

Huber sprang from the trench, received good luck wishes from his co-workers, and hurried off in Duchkar's truck for Sterlington, where the laboring Marie was now in the care of Bessie Shepard McInnis, another older sister of Huber. Bessie's profession was what might be referred to as a nurse midwife: she had formal training as a nurse, but also had acquired many of the skills practiced by physicians. The latter expertise, so valuable in rural areas with few doctors, she acquired by working for years alongside her late first husband, Dr. J. B. Williams. How fortunate were Marie and Huber, living far out in Ouachita Parish, to have a family member in medical practice in the nearest town. As he bounced along the dirt road, Huber wondered how far along Marie might be.

After the trip of less than an hour that seemed like forever, he rolled up to Bessie's house, which also served as her clinic. Even before he shut off the truck, his twelve-year-old niece Elizabeth bounded out of the house and gleefully informed him that he had become a father. Although he had missed the delivery, this was the finest news a man could receive. He was overwhelmed with mixed feelings of apprehension and joy.

Huber entered the house and found Ruth Duchkar beaming at the door of the clinic room. Ruth was also a nurse, yet another of the Shepard family involved in health care. He entered, and laid eyes on his first child in the arms of his wife. They had already decided on the names Van if a boy (to honor Marie's family, the Van Dusens) or Jean if a girl, with each carrying their parent's given name as a middle name.

After gazing speechless for a few moments, Huber would hold his son, Van Huber Shepard, for the first time.

One of the early significant events in Van Shepard's young life would be moving to the nearby city of Monroe as an infant. His father had never intended to make a career of the dangerous gas field work; over the years, he had sustained multiple injuries on the job, which on separate occasions had cost him an index finger and a sizable piece of flesh out of his forearm. Huber had always been intrigued by the retail business. Further, Marie had business acumen afforded by her high school diploma and her involvement in the bookkeeping of her father's veneer mill business in Arkansas. Huber and Marie decided to use their savings and purchase a general store, at the intersection of DeSiard and Powell Streets on the east side of Monroe. They set up housekeeping in living quarters attached to the back of the store.

This was a prime retail location. DeSiard and Powell were US Highways 80 and 165 respectively; their intersection was one of the busiest in northeast Louisiana. The site would become even more lucrative a few years later: Ouachita Parish Junior College would be established on DeSiard less than a mile to the east. The school would later be called Northeast Junior College of Louisiana State University, and, ultimately, the University of Louisiana at Monroe. The "Shepard's" grocery, dry goods, auto service station, and, later, laundromat enterprise would thrive at this location for decades.

It was not long before the family began to grow. Shortly after moving to Monroe, on 22 March 1926, daughter Jean Marie was born to Huber and Marie. "Baby Jean" was followed on 22 February 1927 by William Louis. "Billy" was the third male in the family to carry this name: Huber's father was William Louis Shepard, whose firstborn, in turn, was William Louis Jr. Each had died within a few years of the other at the family homestead near Natchez, Mississippi, when Huber was a young child.

But tragedy was to strike the family soon after Billy's birth. Jean contracted pneumonia in the spring of 1927, possibly brought on by record-setting flooding of the Mississippi River. So extensive was the inundation that at one point much of the land between Monroe and Vicksburg, Mississippi, more than sixty miles to the east, was under water. The Shepard property remained dry on relatively high ground, but many areas in Monroe flooded, and sickness and disease became commonplace. Sadly, Van lost his little sister on the 14th of June, 1927.

In time the Shepards would find themselves in need of more living space for their family, as well as additional retail space for their store. To provide for both, they built a separate home in the late 1920s, on a lot immediately east of the store, at 3400 DeSiard Street. Quite spacious for the day, the home featured two bedrooms, a large living room and country kitchen, and full plumbing and electricity. The space they vacated provided immediate benefits as additional inventory and storage space for the retail operation.

In this same time frame, Marie began to find it difficult to keep up with her duties at the store while serving as mom to Van and Billy. The retail business was growing, requiring ever more of her bookkeeping diligence. In the meantime, the boys were becoming active youngsters, and would not be starting school for years yet. Marie, ever the perfectionist, felt that she could no longer perform either of her roles to her satisfaction. She and Huber began to discuss the possibility of taking on resident child care and homemaking help. Having someone to look after the boys during the day, prepare meals, do laundry, etc., would free Marie to not only continue to manage the books for the business, but to help with the buying and selling as well.

Just as they began to think about advertising for help, a solution presented itself. They were referred to a woman who had lost her husband, and was in need of establishing a situation for herself and her daughter. It was not long before Beulah Bell, with four-year-old Catherine, came to work for the Shepards. She moved into a separate small house on property the Shepards owned, right behind the store. It was an ideal situation: Beulah's homemaking skills proved to be very good, and Catherine, the same age as Van, was an excellent playmate for the boys.

With Marie's life in better balance now, the family began to prosper. Revenues trended upward at Shepard's. For most of 1928 and 1929, life in general was wonderful in these United States, including Louisiana. The gas field continued to produce ever greater quantities of natural gas, and to provide more and more jobs in Ouachita Parish. Agribusiness was also becoming lucrative, especially with cotton, in the rich river bottom lands east of Monroe, all the way to the Mississippi. As an outcome of the 1927 flood, the federal government was engaged in the construction of a system of flood control, via extensive use of levees and dams. Cotton would emerge as the big winner as a result of the more dependable growing conditions. The bullish economy, with its "can't lose" mentality, seemed to pervade northeast Louisiana, just as it did the rest of the country.

However, this type of unbridled boom, propped up by so much human emotion, has a tendency to end suddenly. Never was this more true than with the 1920s period of prosperity. The stock market crash in October 1929 sent the country into an unprecedented economic tailspin, including northeast Louisiana.

Huber and Marie were immediately concerned about what the downturn would mean for their young but growing enterprise, and for their ability to provide for their burgeoning family. But their thrifty nature, and diligent oversight of their business, would serve them well throughout the ensuing depression. They began to more carefully and continuously balance their inventories, to match declining demand.

Huber developed a fierce loyalty to his customers during this difficult time, and they, in turn, to him. He would quietly extend credit to the most trusted. He would patronize the businesses of those that were customers of Shepard's, while stubbornly avoiding those who did their shopping elsewhere.

While their income would be reduced significantly, the enterprise remained profitable. The family purse strings were tightened in accordance, and the Shepards would fare better than most. Indeed, there was never a time that they were unable to pay their bills or have food on the table. They were even able to retain Beulah's domestic services without interruption.

TWO

This Kid Likes Airplanes!

Billy and Van, ca 1935

THROUGHOUT HIS PRESCHOOL YEARS, Van Shepard was a healthy and active child; he busied himself with books, outdoor exploration in his neighborhood, and games with his younger brother and Catherine. As they got older, the children were permitted to be in the store, provided they stayed out of the way, behaved themselves, and respected the inventory. Van was particularly attracted to the service station, which was located in front of the store, under a canopy typical of the period. It was there that he became comfortable with "things mechanical", through the various cars and trucks frequenting the business for fuel, fluids, maintenance, or light repair.

It was also at this time that young Van began to gaze skyward. During certain seasons, the skies around Monroe, Louisiana were as busy as any in the country, with high demand for crop dusting services on the surrounding cotton fields. So lucrative was this business in the area that the largest, Huff Daland Dusters, Inc., relocated its headquarters from Georgia to Monroe in 1925. The company was renamed Delta Air Service in 1928, and soon thereafter initiated regional air mail and passenger service. In time, company founder C. E. Woolman came to patronize Shepard's for groceries and gasoline. Today, the company is known as Delta Air Lines, the largest airline in the world ranked by assets.

Monroe had a municipal airfield which happened to be located about a mile and a half from the Shepards' home. It was thus common for Van and his family to see, and especially hear, the dusters heading out in the morning, and returning for fuel and crop-dust throughout the day. Indeed, Van was fascinated with, even consumed by, airplanes and aviation throughout his childhood. There are many family stories and photographs describing this fascination.

Van Shepard started school in the fall of 1930 at Sherrouse Grammar School in Monroe, just a few blocks from home. He learned and progressed easily in school, despite the distraction of airplanes passing over the schoolhouse, which was even closer to the airfield than the Shepards' home was. While he liked school, he was usually eager to get home and play with Billy or hang around the station.

THE TIPTOEING VALKYRIE

While Van was in first grade, a third son was welcomed into the Shepard household: Samuel Edgar was born on 5 January 1931. Sam was named for Huber's older brother of the same name, who had died ten years earlier near their boyhood home in Mississippi.

Sustained by the strong work ethic of Huber and Marie, the family continued to survive into the depths of the Great Depression, even thriving in terms relative to the times. There was little in way of recreation or diversion in those days: all was focused toward survival, "noses to the grindstone". The family never had a real vacation until much later. There were always long hours in the store and station, including on weekends.

Thus there could be long hours for Beulah Bell as well. Plus a toddler to look after now! This was especially challenging for her in the afternoons, if Van, now in second grade, were around the house after school. At this time Beulah had also wanted to be nearer her family downstate. An opportunity emerged to take a similar home-making position there, and, reluctantly, she took leave of the Shepards, and headed south with Catherine.

This left the Shepards in dire need of a new caregiver for the boys. And the need would get more pressing: Marie was expecting yet another child.

They were again blessed with a wonderful, ready-made solution to their problem. Huber had hired Fred McCollum, a black man, to help him operate the station, so that he could focus more on the grocery's needs. Fred proved to be a valuable asset to the enterprise: in addition to good mechanical aptitude, he had excellent rapport with the black community, and well-earned respect from the white. He was largely responsible for an increase in the number of regular black customers at the store.

It turns out that Fred's wife, Merlene, was already looking to find employment, not an easy thing to do in the midst of the depression. When she learned of the departure of Beulah Bell, she and Fred proposed that she assume Beulah's caregiver duties, with the couple moving into the servants' quarters that Beulah and Catherine had vacated. Huber and Marie were already acquainted with Merlene, and thought highly of her. It seemed like a match made in heaven, with Merlene able to care for the boys and Fred continuing, and even expanding, his role at the station.

Van and Billy, though they would miss the Bells, were very comfortable with Merlene, and they had already grown to love Fred. They thought the whole notion was grand.

The family was thus well positioned to welcome the addition of a new little sister to the boys: Frances Marie, born 16 October 1932. She was given the same names as her mother, but was called by her first name (actually "Sis" by nearly everyone) to distinguish her from Marie.

Family life was important to the Shepards. Despite both parents working long hours in the store and station, they made a priority of dining together when the work was done, and bonding further there-after. Listening to radio programs was a frequent family endeavor in the evenings. Marie would proudly remind the children that the wood veneer in their radio cabinet was provided by her father's business, Van Veneer Company, in Arkansas.

On Sunday mornings, Marie and the children, and sometimes Huber as well, would worship, at the First Methodist Church, and later at Memorial Methodist Church. Marie would remain a member at one or the other for more than sixty years.

Later on Sundays were the occasional visits with Huber's three nearby siblings and their families. There were the aforementioned older sisters Bessie McInnis (in Sterlington) and Ruth Duchkar (in Monroe), each married with children. Huber, the youngest of nine, also had a brother Claude living in Monroe with his wife Ella and their three children. Claude was an employee of the railroad. Early on, these two families would get together just as the others did.

However, at some point Huber may have felt that Claude's family was not doing enough of their shopping at Shepard's. The two brothers, who had been close in childhood (they were only three years apart), had a falling out which, sadly, would last the rest of their days. Despite the estrangement, on a few occasions Marie would take the kids, without Huber, to visit Claude, Ella, and their children Claude Jr., Mabel, and Becky.

Huber's oldest sister, Daisy Frost, was the only sibling still living in Mississippi. She and her husband Edward raised several children in the Natchez area. They still owned "Walnut Grove", the original sixty acre Shepard homestead ten miles north of Natchez, where Huber and all of his siblings were born and raised. Daisy and Huber maintained a relationship, but seldom saw each other given the distance between their homes.

The Shepards also remained close with Marie's family in Arkansas, which was even larger than Huber's. Marie was the third of ten children born to Harry and Lillie Van Dusen. When Marie was twelve, her family had moved from her Ohio birthplace to Arkansas. There Harry launched his successful wood veneer business, taking advantage of the plentiful forests of the various wood species that are used for veneer. Almost all of the Van Dusen children were involved in the business at one time or another. Demand for veneer in American industry was great, as it was used in many products consumed by the growing population, such as cabinetry, baskets, and seating. One company claim-to-fame was the supply of veneer for the seatbacks in the original 1923 Yankee Stadium in New York.

But the Great Depression hit the Van Dusens hard, as it did most working-class Americans. Van Veneer nearly had to close its doors, and many employees were let go. Savings were lost in failed banks. But the family persevered, many taking on outside work and multiple jobs to make ends meet. Some hunted in order to help keep food on the table.

Some family members rekindled a skill developed back in their

Ohio days: basketweaving. They would gather scraps from the veneer milling process, and weave them into beautiful baskets for sale as shopping baskets, baby swing seats, etc. Even the children would contribute to the effort. Many Van Dusen baskets still grace the homes of descendants today.

Throughout the hard times, the Van Dusens never wavered on their family priorities. Slowly but surely they reestablished the viability of Van Veneer and returned to a state of normalcy.

The Shepards would usually spend Christmas in Arkansas, at the rambling Van Dusen home on the north side of the town of Malvern. The holidays were always a grand affair: by 1935, there were no less than 54 descendants and spouses of Harry & Lillie, and most of them would be home for Christmas. As many lived in Malvern, there was always accommodation available for those from out of town.

The Shepards would keep their businesses open on Christmas Eve, and would thus be among the last to arrive in Malvern. Their arrival would always be eagerly anticipated by the others, particularly the youngsters, who would have a great time reconnecting and romping with their cousins. But all too soon, the Shepards would have to head back to Monroe, to literally get back to business.

During the summer, one of the Shepard kids would occasionally get to spend extended time in Malvern. Later on, the Van Dusens would purchase a camp a few miles away on the north shore of Lake Catherine, a reservoir upstream on the Ouachita River (which ironically flowed down to Monroe, Louisiana). The camp featured several cabins, and proved to be a popular getaway and reunion site, for both those living in Malvern as well as out-of-towners. It was a wonderful and memorable spot for the children.

THREE

Hangin' at Selman

Van Shepard, ca 1940

I T WAS NOT LONG before aviation would begin to take an even firmer grip on Van Shepard. As soon as he was old enough to pedal a bike, he would leverage this newfound mobility to further indulge in his passion. Once he completed his chores around the house and at the store, he would often ride out to the airfield to watch the crop dusters return from their day's work. This became a years-long ritual. He would marvel at the skills shown by the pilots, later describing them as a daring group that flew by instinct. Watching them work the fields, diving and swooping just above the cotton tassels, was as good as any air show!

Van enjoyed those Sunday visits with Aunt Bessie's family in Sterlington: one of her sons, Norman "Mack Jr" McInnis, was five years Van's senior and likewise interested in aviation. He and Van would talk airplanes for hours during these visits. Van was envious of Mack's general knowledge of aviation as the "older kid", while Mack was envious of Van's living so close to the airfield. The boys fed off each other's passion, each pledging to the other to become a pilot someday.

Van also had a close associate on his mother's side, who would indulge him on every one of his trips to Malvern. Clyde Erwin Van Dusen, the eldest child of Marie's brother Clyde, was also consumed by airplanes. Just as Van did with Mack Jr back in Louisiana, he and Clyde Erwin, three years older, would get into diligent discussion on the latest in airplanes and aviation.

In addition to watching the dusters and engaging his cousins, Van began reading and rereading everything he could find about airplanes. He had now moved on to the excellent and relatively new Neville High School on Monroe's north side. The school librarian had picked up on his passion, and could see the potential for aviation to become a career for him. She was happy to feed him with a few titles she was able to obtain. One in particular, *I Wanted Wings* by Beirne Lay, Jr., he would later admit to reading a dozen times.

By the age of fifteen, Van was beginning to spend more time at the airfield, which had been expanded over the years. It was now known as Selman Field, named for US Navy pilot Augustus Selman, a Monroe native who died in an airplane crash in 1921. More than just watching the crop dusters flying in, Van was developing a rapport with the people and machinery around the facility. He would surprise the various pilots and mechanics with the breadth of his knowledge of airplanes.

One of the businesses operating out of Selman was the flight school of "Pappy" Severance. Pappy used the Piper Cub, one of the most successful trainer aircraft in aviation history. Inevitably, Van began to bug Pappy about getting a ride in his Cub. Pappy's answer was always the same: "Three dollars for five minutes." Van decided that he would have to come up with the three dollars, quite a sum for a schoolkid at the end of the depression.

By this time Van was on the payroll at Shepard's, being paid a princely ten cents an hour for his time at the store and station. Most of this he used to buy gasoline, for those few times he was allowed to use his father's 1929 Ford Model A (in which he also made grocery deliveries for the store). While they notionally approved of the idea, Van knew that his "economically strict" parents would require him to earn his way into such a discretionary expense as an airplane ride. Thus he began to save virtually all of his earnings, figuring it should take about a month to accumulate the three dollars.

After several weeks, Van had learned another of life's lessons: saving on a limited income is a hard thing to do. Despite his best efforts, he had only put away half of his required sum. He would have to scrimp even harder.

At that time young Sam had been after his brother to take him along on his visits to Selman. Van relented, and the boys rode their bikes out to the field. As they were gaping at Pappy's airplane, Van was authoritatively educating Sam on the attributes of the Cub. Pappy spotted them, came out, and asked how Van's savings were coming. When he replied with the less-than-stellar news, Pappy decided he'd make the boys an offer they couldn't refuse: if they would give the Cub a good washing, he would take them each for a ride in it for the $1.50.

After about a half hour, never was an airplane so spotless! Pappy took Van and then Sam each up for a loop around the field. Each brother would remember the experience for the rest of his life. In

Van's case, in his own words, he would "eat, sleep, and dream airplanes" from then on.

About this time, World War II had broken out in Europe. The topic of the day was whether or not the United States should enter the war in support of the Allies. While virtually everyone of age in the country was on edge with the situation, it did have the effect of causing them to forget about the recent years of tough economic times, and look more forward, to whatever was coming next.

One tangible effect of the onset of war was the government's realization, should the US indeed enter the war, that there were not enough qualified pilots across the country. It had taken a long time, but air power had finally been acknowledged as vitally important to any first-world nation's ability to defend in time of war. The US could create the needed aircraft manufacturing capacity (it had indeed been ramping up production to meet lend-lease commitments to the United Kingdom and other allies), but it would not have enough pilots to fly its own planes without extraordinary action.

This situation had not gone unnoticed by President Franklin Roosevelt. He authorized the creation of the Civilian Pilot Training Program (CPTP), which intended to increase the pool of qualified pilots available to the military, should there be a national emergency such as war declaration. The program, launched in large scale in 1939, used junior colleges and civilian flight schools throughout the country to turn out these contingency pilots. Both Northeast Junior College of LSU and Severance's Flight School in Monroe were integrally involved in the CPTP. Indeed, "Mack Jr" McInnis received his pilot's license through the program in 1940 while a student at Northeast. How envious was Van on those occasions he was able to watch his older cousin take flight instruction at Selman!

Van graduated from Neville High School in the spring of 1941, at the age of 16 1/2 (Neville did not add a twelfth grade until later). He enrolled at Northeast, whose campus was even closer to the family's house than Neville High was. He intended to follow in Mack Jr's footsteps, and pursue his pilot's license through the CPTP at Northeast. However, he was crushed upon learning that the minimum age for CPTP enrollment was 18. He would have to postpone his plans.

The delay toward his dream was not all bad for Van, although this was hard for him to see right away. It enabled him to focus on his studies at Northeast, without the distraction of learning to fly at the same time. Further, he was able to work more hours at Shepard's, bolstering his savings accordingly.

In lieu of formal flight instruction, Van would continue to hang out at Selman, absorbing all that he could from the myriad aviation activity underway there. Now, in addition to cropdusting, passenger air travel, and other commercial endeavor, Selman was host to booming CPTP flight instruction activity. Van worked out a deal with Pappy Severance: in exchange for odd jobs such as washing and moving planes around, sweeping the office floor, etc., he could listen in on some of the instruction, and even bum the occasional ride. He reveled in the opportunity to take the controls on some of these flights, and found flying to be natural to his instincts. It wasn't quite the real thing, and none of it would count toward it, but it kept Van's passion for aviation growing.

Then, the Day of Infamy. Sunday, 7 December 1941: the day that was indelibly etched on the minds of all Americans of that generation. The Shepards were enjoying a Sunday afternoon together at home, when news of the Pearl Harbor attack came over the radio. Everyone, even nine-year-old Sis, sat in stunned silence as the details of the devastation began to trickle in throughout the day.

War was now certain, and made official by President Roosevelt on Monday. All over town and on the Northeast campus, emotions of every sort poured forth, over what was ahead for all Americans. Van, his classmates, and especially the "pilots-to-be" knew that their time would certainly come. But there were many speeches from those in positions of leadership, to the effect that all Americans should, first and foremost, keep doing what they were doing, only better. So everyone went about their business, only with a bit more purpose. For Van this meant studying ever harder, and working ever harder at the store, as his father so sternly lectured him.

The family spent Christmas again in Arkansas, but it was different this time, with an air of sadness instead of frivolity, but also one of resolve. Several young Van Dusen men or husbands had enlisted, or were planning to. Van's cousin Clyde Erwin, 20, was planning to continue at the University of Arkansas for one more semester, and then join the Marines for pilot school.

And war meant that Selman Field was to change radically. It had already become a busy place by 1942 with the CPTP underway, but that was nothing compared to what was coming that summer: the Army Air Forces decided that the field would be strategically important to its mission, and assumed control on 17 June 1942, creating Selman Army Airfield. The plan was for Selman to become a principal navigator school for the AAF. Construction was immediate and rapid on runways and facilities to accommodate the students, instructors, pilots, and aircraft. A trio of 6,100 foot concrete runways was constructed to the east of the existing shorter strips; these runways remain in use today as Monroe Regional Airport. In time, Selman became the largest navigator school in the country, and the only one in which a student could go through all phases of training and get his navigator wings at the same facility. By war's end over fifteen thousand men will have graduated there, more than half of the AAF's total.

This change was not good news for Van Shepard. Due to the buildup of the navigator school, there would be no more CPTP training at Selman. His plans for flight school through the CPTP were dashed for the second time in less than a year. Van thought long and hard about whether he should continue at Northeast, versus enlisting as soon as he turned 18 in October. His cousin Mack Jr, now 22, had dropped out of Louisiana State University in Baton Rouge, enlisted in the Navy, and already received his pilot's wings. It seemed to Van that something was always pulling the plug on his plans to become a pilot. However, sound reasoning prevailed and he decided to continue, as he could complete his studies at Northeast only six months later anyway, and then enlist with a two-year college diploma in hand.

About this time, the exploits of Colonel Claire Chennault's "Flying Tigers", three squadrons of volunteer American fighter pilots battling the Japanese for air supremacy in China, were coming to light in news reports. Van had heard that Colonel Chennault was from Louisiana. When a feature article on him appeared in Life magazine in August 1942, Van learned that not only was he raised in Louisiana, but just down the road in the town of Gilbert, about an hour from Monroe; he was, in fact, married in Winnsboro, even closer. What is more, the Flying Tigers were featured in a Hollywood movie of the same name starring John Wayne; Van would see it multiple times. For years thereafter, he would follow Chennault's activities in China with special interest.

By early 1943, the war had entered its darkest period for the United States and the Allies – successes were few and setbacks many, in both the European and Pacific theaters. Strict conservation measures had been applied for all US residents, such as rationing of gasoline and other consumables, and even switching the metal in pennies to steel, in order to save copper for shell casings. US industry had switched over the manufacture of its normal products to wartime production, making all manner of products for the military, from mess kits to aircraft. The ranks of the armed forces were burgeoning daily, with both enlistees and those selected by the newly instituted national draft.

This sense of urgency affected everyone in the country, including Van Shepard. He would graduate from Northeast Junior College of LSU with his two-year diploma in May. Well before the end of classes, he had visited the US Navy recruitment office in Monroe, intending to enlist and attain his pilot's wings as soon as possible.

During the enlistment interview process, a series of general health questions were posed. These would pre-screen candidates in advance of the full physical that all would be required to pass later, in order to be accepted for service. Van had long dealt with a mild case of asthma, which in reality was more of a bother than a medical condition. It had never required treatment, and was not so severe as to require the use of a rescue inhaler. In fact, Van had played baseball all through high school and college, with no effect on his performance.

He dutifully noted this history in his Navy health survey. Little did he realize that this alone would be sufficient to disqualify him as a pilot candidate. Yet again, he was turned away from his dream.

Anguished about his situation as he was, Van was indisposed to joining his fellow graduates in regaling their last days at Northeast. Taking the advice of others that were enlisting, he adopted a new strategy. Diploma in hand, he would visit the Army recruiting office this time, targeting the Army Air Forces as the vehicle to achieve his dreams, and conceal his asthma condition in the pre-screening process. He would then hope for the best during the subsequent full physical.

He developed an excellent rapport with the Army recruiter, who seemed more impressed with his broad knowledge of aviation than the Navy recruiter was. He passed his pre-screening, and reported with enthusiasm, yet also some apprehension, to the recruiting depot in Shreveport a few days later. He never mentioned his asthma condition, which was mild enough that it never manifested itself in the breathing assessments administered by the medical personnel. He passed all of his exams, and Van Huber Shepard became aviation cadet #38391598 in the US Army Air Forces on 21 May 1943.

FOUR

"You're in the Army (Air Forces) Now"

As AAF cadet, 1943

I N THE SUMMER OF 1943, the AAF was dealing with its massive influx of aviation cadets. It was a multi-faceted challenge: not only did the recruits have to be taught to fly, but all the rudiments of being a soldier in wartime had to be learned. Though moving fast in creating suitable new facilities, the Army simply lacked sufficient space to immediately house and train all of its pilots-to-be. In order to avoid having to idle new recruits, and the morale problems that would ensue, it partnered with colleges and universities to establish a new concept called College Training Detachments (CTD). This program utilized college facilities and nearby airfields to educate newly recruited aviation cadets over several months, until there was capacity at the AAF flight schools.

With its well established Reserve Officers' Training Corps (ROTC) programs and its proximity to Selman Army Airfield, Northeast Junior College of LSU was an ideal choice as an early launch site of the CTD program. Van Shepard had assumed that CTD would be his destiny, and was indeed assigned to the program at Northeast. He reported to campus on 4 June 1943. While it was a bit of a letdown to return to the same facilities he had frequented for the prior two years, he understood the situation, and took heart in the fact that he would now be paid for doing many of the same things he did as a college student. Further, holding a two-year college diploma, he was credited for some of the non-aviation courses that were required of others, and could immediately proceed with aviation-related electives such as navigation, meteorology, and air traffic control. He was told he would accordingly have early access to openings at the AAF flight schools.

For most of the "pre-cadets", the highlight of the CTD program was the ten hours of flight experience included at Selman. While not much more than a ride-along program, this element nonetheless succeeded in providing indoctrination and maintaining enthusiasm for the recruits until they could get to the "real thing". In Van's particular case, this was a bit less valuable, as he had already spent time flying out of the same field and even the same type of aircraft, the Piper Cub. But he accepted the experience as a plus to the program, and attacked his studies diligently.

Throughout the somewhat boring summer, Van easily passed his various tests and examinations. Then, the wire he so impatiently awaited arrived on 4 October 1943 (his nineteenth birthday!): he was to report for Pre-Flight school at the AAF's San Antonio Aviation Cadet Center (SAACC) on 12 October.

Van packed those few things he would be able to bring with him, said goodbye to his loved ones, and boarded a bus for SAACC, in south central Texas. He and his fellow newly arriving cadets immediately went through a one-week classification stage, in which they were given traditional orientation, haircutting, bunk assignments, etc. Somewhat predictably, Van would take on the nickname "Shep", which would follow him throughout his aviation career. The cadets then went into classroom examinations to establish their knowledge of physics and basic aviation principles, to ensure their readiness to become pilots. Given his college diploma and CTD experience, Van had little trouble attaining high marks in these assessments, and his entry into the ten-week Pre-Flight stage was almost a formality.

The first six weeks of Pre-Flight was basically a "boot camp for pilots", teaching military discipline and demeanor, fitness training, drill instruction and marching, pistol shooting, and the like. The cadets noticed that due to the rapid gearup, full base readiness was a work in progress. There were many incidents of running out of certain foods during mess, electrical and plumbing infrastructure issues, etc. Van was not issued his uniform until almost four weeks after his arrival. It took a while for him to feel like he was a part of the American military juggernaut.

At the end of "boot camp", the cadets were allowed to send and receive mail. In one letter from home, Van received some news that profoundly affected him. His cousin Clyde Erwin Van Dusen, by then a 22-year-old Lieutenant pilot in the Marines, had ditched his carrier-based dive bomber in the Pacific, and was declared missing in action and presumed dead. He was the first serviceman from Malvern, Arkansas to be killed in action in World War II. Van would enter his first meaningful pilot training with a heavy heart, but also with renewed commitment not only to his country but to the memory of his cousin.

Pre-Flight moved into more specific aviation instruction during the last four weeks. This started with classroom academics or "ground school", paralleled with time in the "Link Trainer". This device was a simple box-like flight simulator that provided somewhat realistic response to elevator, aileron, and rudder inputs. It was used not only to allow most cadets their first experience with aircraft control response, but enabled instructors to weed out those that were clearly in over their heads with the idea of becoming a pilot. While Van welcomed this new aid to his learning, it would be a rare session in which he felt he was learning anything new.

At long last, it was on to the indoctrination flights. The cadets were given the chance to ride in two-place trainers with flight instructors. This proceeded on a daily basis for a week or more, and was a very real introduction to flying: the cadets flew in full gear including parachutes, and once aloft would take the stick from the first flight.

Part of the intent of these flights was to wash out those that lacked either basic flying instincts or the stomach required, or simply didn't have the nerve. Accordingly, the cadets were subjected to high-G maneuvers in later indoctrination flights. Here again, with Van Shepard's prior experience, he was ahead of many of his fellow cadets. Even though these aircraft were larger and more powerful than the Piper Cubs he had flown in, he easily handled all that his instructor could dish out, and was summarily promoted to the next stage, Primary, by Christmas 1943.

Primary flight school meant a change of venue for Van. Due to the volume of flight training underway in the war, many civilian schools had to be contracted by the USAAF to provide Primary for the student pilots. Those schools associated with the San Antonio Aviation Cadet Center were in Texas or nearby states. Van was designated for the school at Cimarron Field, west of Oklahoma City. He arrived there between Christmas and New Year's Day, and settled in for the ten-week stage. His mount for Primary would be the Fairchild PT-19 Cornell, a single-engine, low-wing, open cockpit trainer. The "PT" designator indicated "Primary Trainer". He progressed steadily through the stage, learning all the basic flying maneuvers as taught by his instructor.

At this time, Van learned from home with sadness that Fred and Merlene, the family's trusted employees, had decided to move to California, where a job awaited Fred at a defense plant. The McCollums had wanted to improve their lot, and, furthermore, the Shepard children were now all old enough to care for themselves after school, if not in fact be working in the store. They would nonetheless miss Fred and Merlene, and would forever hold them in high esteem as "second parents" who had a lasting impact on their upbringing.

Back at Cimarron, the training was becoming more intense, both in ground school and in the air. While Van continued to relish the experience, more than a few of the cadets were beginning to struggle with the rigors of the course, and many would "wash out" by the end of the stage. But Van continued to develop his skills steadily. By early April he had accrued 65 hours, 15 minutes of Primary flight time, and was promoted to Basic.

The Basic stage of pilot training would represent quite a change for Van. He moved from the civilian facility at Cimarron Field to the Army Airfield at Garden City, Kansas on Saturday, 15 April 1944. He had enjoyed a few comforts at the civilian operation that would be "gone with the wind" in Kansas, as described in a letter to home on his second day:

Well, I am now back in the Army, and I do mean the Army. Primary was a Country Club Deluxe compared to this place. The discipline is very strict, "at attention" in the mess halls, etc. I sure would like to see a natural gas heater: these barracks are tar paper shacks with coal stoves, and we have to keep them burning. They are always out in the morning and I really freeze; it takes quite a while to start a coal fire. The latrines are about 200 ft from the barracks.

Letter from Garden City Army Airfield, 17 April 1944

During the first week at Basic the cadets were assigned a class number, which remained with them through the end of Advanced when they (hopefully) would receive their wings. Van was assigned 44-H, corresponding to the eighth class initiated at Garden City in 1944. At this point the cadets expressed a preference for single-engine or multi-engine, according to what type of flying they wanted to focus their training toward. The single-engine group would orient toward the smaller pursuit aircraft, and the multi-engine group toward the larger bombers and cargo aircraft. But there were no guarantees: graduates would be turned out not only according to needs for each type in the operating theaters, but according to what the instructors felt each cadet's skills were best suited for. Van declared his preference for single-engine.

Normally both ground school and flying began immediately. However, 44-H's flying was weathered out until the second week, so Van had to fly weekends to catch up. His ride for the ten weeks of Basic was the Vultee BT-13 Valiant ("BT" for Basic Trainer). This was a low-wing closed-cockpit tandem trainer, with the cadet's first exposure to landing flaps and a variable pitch propeller. Notably, it also featured a radial engine of about 450 horsepower, more than twice the power of the PT-19 used in Primary. One of the first jobs of the instructors was to prevent the cadets from getting overly exuberant with all that power, and instead respect the danger that comes with it.

The 4th of May 1944 was a big day for Van Shepard: he soloed in the BT-13. After his second such flight, he was cleared for unsupervised solo flight for the remainder of the stage. His focus then moved to aerial acrobatics, learning any number of advanced maneuvers, some with fancy names like the Chandelle and the Immelmann.

One of the exercises later given the cadets was to prepare them for extensive cross-country flying coming up in their training. Van describes one such exercise:

> This map reading ride includes two or three buzz jobs of railroad stations to find out the name of the town. Our instructors show us how to do it in case we get lost on our cross-country. You go down to about 1000 ft and find out where all the obstructions and high tension lines are, then start letting down away from the town to about 200 ft, and then turn over the railroad tracks and start for the station. When you get close to the station, you get down to about 75 ft and read the name of the town. Boy, that was the most fun I've had since I have been flying!
>
> Letter from Garden City Army Airfield, 17 May 1944

While Van continued to grade satisfactorily, the general level of stress in the class continued to build. The demands of both academics and flying performance were so constant and heavy that many cadets began to crack. Two of Van's classmates heavily damaged their aircraft during rough landings. Later, another, who had the same instructor as Van, was killed while soloing in an unwitnessed crash fifteen miles from the field. Needless to say, these incidents had a sobering effect on all the cadets. And adding to the stress level was the start of instrument training. This entailed classroom work, Link trainer time, and flight time under "the hood", a black curtain surrounding the student so that he must rely only on his instruments to fly the plane. Van characterized instrument flying as, by far, the most difficult aspect he had encountered to date. He so struggled at one point, that, for the first time, he began to have doubts about his ability to pass Basic. His instructor was hard on him, berating him for every little error he made.

It was now June 1944. The news from the Allied D-Day invasion on the sixth, and in the days following, dominated the attention of everyone at Garden City Army Airfield. Just as it had with Pearl Harbor, the news had people reaching back for a bit more in their daily endeavor. For Van, it served to further motivate him and sharpen his focus on his instrument training.

Night flying soon followed the instrument training. Towards the end of Basic, the cadets were flying nightly both with instructors and solo. Included were many practice landings, with various combinations of illumination: aircraft landing lights, runway floods, runway markers only. Mixed in with the nighttime exercises were three daytime cross-country trips, and the cadets' first exercises in formation flying. Back on the ground, Van would also practice both pistol and machine gun shooting on occasion, in which he generally achieved good marks.

On 24 June 1944 Van received good news and bad news. The good: he passed Basic. The bad: his next and final stage, Advanced, would be for multi-engine aircraft, not the single-engine he had requested. He was distressed at this, as the pilot he had fancied himself was the high-G, seat-of-the-pants, stick jockey, not the "straight & level" yoke-steering variety. The reasons for the decision were not specified; he wondered if his struggles with instrument flying may have factored in. Nonetheless, he accepted his lot, and forced himself to focus on the positive attributes of flying larger aircraft, such as the feeling of sheer power of multiple engines, and the additional room and comfort afforded by the more spacious cabin. He would launch himself into the Advanced stage with the same eagerness as in the previous stages.

FIVE

Wings!

With B-25 Mitchell, 1945

T HE MULTI-ENGINE DESIGNATES of Class 44-H arrived for Advanced at Pampa Army Airfield, in the Texas panhandle, early on the morning of Friday, 30 June 1944. Physical exams were the first order of business, followed by an act of Army optimism: the cadets were measured for their officer's uniforms, which, presuming their success, they would be issued upon graduation ten weeks hence. In his physical, Van would continue to improve with each eye exam he took, particularly in pilot-critical depth perception.

As with the prior stages, Advanced school featured both class-room and flight time almost daily. In addition, the Link simulator continued to be used, especially for instrument training. The training aircraft was the Cessna AT-17 Bobcat. Also known as the UC-78, the Bobcat was a low-wing, twin radial engine aircraft with fully enclosed cabin. It was known to its pilots as the "Bamboo Bomber". For the cadets, this was their first exposure to retractable main gear, differential use of the engines to assist taxi steering, and flying with pilot and copilot seated side-by-side. Now with 155 flying hours to his credit, Van began flying the Bobcat on his third day at Pampa. For Multi-Engine Advanced, there was less emphasis on acrobatics, and more on formation flying, cross-country, instrument flying, and radio navigation.

Van's family had inquired about the fact that he seemed to be saving almost all of his paychecks. His reply is illuminating:

> Well, if you could see these towns out here in the West, such as Pampa and Garden City, you wouldn't spend much money either. You usually go to town once or twice and then don't go anymore, for you wished that you would have stayed home those two times. That is the reason I save so much money. I know what happened after the last War. It is going to be tough after this War, depression, and so forth. I am going to save as much as I can.
>
> Letter from Pampa Army Airfield, 23 July 1944

Van may have been wrong about a post World War II depression, but his thrifty nature, developed of necessity as a child in the thirties, would serve him well throughout his life. As a pilot, he would earn more than an Army regular of equivalent rank throughout his career, an acknowledgment to the hazardous nature of flying.

One facet of Van's character that would sustain him during the grueling and stressful pilot training experience was his spiritual faith. He was a Christian, coming from a family to whom church and worship were important. Throughout his time in the Air Forces, he was encouraged by his mother to seek out and attend worship services. He was successful with this at Pampa, closing one letter as follows:

> Oh yes, Mom, I went to church this morning. I have been every Sunday except one.
>
> Letter from Pampa Army Airfield, 30 July 1944

Instrument flying continued to be a challenge for Van. Unlike almost all other elements of flying, this one did not come naturally to him. His progress was slow, and as part of his mid-stage examinations in August, he failed his instrument check flight. Given his demonstrated excellence in the other pilot attributes, in lieu of washing him out altogether, his superiors decided to hold him back to class 44-I.

Upon joining 44-I, Van knew well that this would be his last chance to attain his wings. He set about his efforts in the following weeks with renewed focus, putting in extra work on instrument flying, ground school, "under the hood" in the Link simulator, and in the cockpit. His efforts would pay off: he passed his next scheduled instrument check flight on 2 October, and was back in good standing.

Notwithstanding his progress, weather delays had become problematic for Advanced class 44-I. Even flying weekends, the cadets were not projected to accrue their required seventy hours by the 16 October graduation date. As a result, their leadership made the unpopular decision to add five weeks to the stage, to 20 November. Together with his demotion from 44-H, this meant a total of ten extra weeks for Van at Pampa. He hastily changed his post graduation train reservation. One benefit of the change: the extra time seemed to give him more confidence in his ability to graduate.

Another change enabled by the five-week delay for 44-I was the decision to start the cadets on the North American B-25J Mitchell medium bomber. This amounted to a pullahead of what was already planned for the next class: exposure to a bomber that was typical of the type the pilots would transition to for combat, following graduation. Van had mixed emotions about this: he liked the idea of learning to fly a bomber, but felt it represented yet another chance to wash him out, should he find it difficult.

His concern proved to be unfounded. As he felt the engines run up on his first takeoff as copilot, Van couldn't believe he was at the yoke of the very type used in the Doolittle raid on Tokyo, a mere two and a half years earlier. The B-25 was a high-wing, twin-tail design, by far the most powerful Van had piloted to date. It was also his first exposure to tricycle landing gear, all of his previous mounts being "tail-draggers" with a small wheel at the rear of the fuselage. There would thus be new takeoff and landing techniques to learn. But he would find that he and the Mitchell would agree with each other. In short order, his instructor had him doing light acrobatics (such as they are in a bomber), as well as flying on one engine. He found it easy to land and no more difficult to fly on instruments than the trainer. He passed a check flight with flying colors (no pun intended), and would end Advanced with thirty hours in the B-25J.

With each passing day, the cadets were thinking more and more about graduation. Even if successful, there would be one additional decision made for them: assignment either as Second Lieutenant pilot, or as "flight officer". The latter, while carrying the same pay grade, was a non-commissioned position. Flight officers would not be command pilots, but would be involved with other flight operation duties. The graduating classes were about evenly divided into both, but predictably, most of the graduates would prefer the full pilot classification. Because he had been held back from 44-H, Van worried that making Second Lieutenant pilot was going to be a stretch for him. All he could do was to continue to impress and hope for the best. Either way, he'd have those silver wings.

On the last Saturday afternoon of Advanced, Van was apprised by class 44-I leadership that he would receive his pilot's wings on Monday, 20 November 1944, receive his instrument rating, and be commissioned Second Lieutenant pilot O-2074249, US Army Air Forces!

As he lay awake that night in his Pampa barracks one last time, Van Shepard made up his mind that flying airplanes would be his endeavor for life.

Van took the train home to Monroe, to see his family for the first time in thirteen months. It was a wonderful and much needed three week furlough. At this time of the war, his status as an Army Air Forces officer-pilot made him quite the man about town; he was the toast of his buddies, rarely paying for his own drinks. With Monroe's proximity to a facility with thousands of military men, there were many opportunities for entertainment nightly. Van leveraged his new status for female companionship as well. He had many dates with girlfriends old and new.

He also could not resist the temptation to flaunt his new wings at the now-gigantic navigation school at Selman Field. He slipped out to the field several times to rub elbows with the pilots flying the "nav" trainers, some of whom were friends. He enjoyed the contrast of the old runways from his youth, now the site of barracks, with the constant takeoffs and landings on the new runways.

Ever since leaving Pampa, Van had been pondering his next assignment. He knew it would be transition training, the fifteen week immersion on the specific aircraft model the pilot would fly into combat, but he did not know which aircraft it would be. Finally he received a wire ordering him to report on Monday, 11 December 1944 to Laughlin Army Airfield near Del Rio, Texas, for transition on the B-26 Marauder medium bomber. Immediately upon arrival, he began his flying. Like the B-25, the Marauder was also a high-wing, twin radial engine aircraft, but was one which early on had a reputation as a "widowmaker". It had been pressed into service in both the Pacific and European combat theaters in 1942, often with pilots not sufficiently trained. Van defended the Marauder though, in this letter to home:

> I see you all ask how I like the B-26. I think it is a sweet airplane, and all the talk you hear about it being a "flying coffin" is misleading. It is a fact [that] lots get killed in them in the States, but I think, in fact, it is the most strongly built twin-engine airplane made. A damn good airplane for combat; "she'll bring you home."
>
> Letter from Laughlin Army Airfield, 31 December 1944

It is indeed well documented that changes accommodated in later B-26 variants, together with better crew training, led to loss rates well below those of other US combat aircraft.

Van's burgeoning "need for speed" was satisfied by this bomber, which was thirty miles per hour faster than his ride at Pampa, the B-25. But with this speed came increased danger. The Marauder's landing speed was commensurately fast, and could indeed be a handful for novice pilots accustomed to the more forgiving Mitchell. But Van would never be intimidated by speed in his mounts, and managed the Marauder well.

By January, his training would move to the night shift, with ground school starting at 7:00 pm and flying at 1:00 am. This freed up his days, which he began to take advantage of. He would often take leave to Del Rio, enjoying crossing the border into Ciudad

Acuña, Mexico, for shopping. Even picking up a little Spanish, he began to cultivate an appreciation for the Latin culture that would follow him for the rest of his life.

In this winter of 1944-45, Van began to take increasing interest in the accomplishments of his brother Bill (no longer called "Billy") back home. Bill had followed in his older brother's footsteps, and would be finishing up his own two-year diploma at Northeast Junior College of LSU in the spring. Also interested in aviation, he was planning to enlist in the US Navy, and thinking about pilot school. In the meantime, he was very involved in Northeast's ROTC program, attaining its Commandant position. Van, in his letters home, would often encourage and counsel him. Bill passed his Navy entrance exams, graduated from Northeast in April 1945, and entered service at the Naval Air Technical Training Center in Millington, Tennessee, near Memphis. The Shepard family now had two boys in uniform, each in their respective service's aviation corps.

It was at this time that the Allies began to have the Axis powers on the run in Europe. Back in the States, the daily news reports detailed success after success on just about every front. The mood was upbeat in both the civilian and military ranks. There was a side effect, though, in the various Army Air Forces transition schools preparing their new pilots for combat: rather suddenly, there was not the priority in these operations that there was in years past. The schools were having to deal with reduced deliveries of aviation fuel and aircraft parts, as well as receiving battle-scarred aircraft returning from the combat theaters as trainers. Some venues were being drawn down completely, their training operations consolidated elsewhere. Van noted that the pace of activity at Laughlin was slowing. His transition program had been extended indefinitely beyond the original fifteen weeks.

One good outcome of the slowdown for Van was that many pilots were allowed to begin flying other available aircraft types at Laughlin. He seized the opportunity to check out in the North American AT-6 Texan ("AT" for Advanced Trainer), the powerful pursuit trainer which he would have flown in the Advanced stage of pilot school, had he been designated for single-engine. He relished the chance to keep his higher performance skillset in development via this program, and took all the AT-6 hours he could get.

On 20 April 1945, he was invited to ferry AT-6A #41-16519 the short distance from Laughlin to Randolph Field, Texas, near the aviation cadet center where he started his career. He jumped at the chance. What he did not know was that the exercise would end with the first flying incident of his nascent career. Following an uneventful 160 mile flight to Randolph, after touchdown he "ground-looped" the Texan, the aviation equivalent of the "spinout". It could have been worse: while he grounded a wingtip, the plane was not significantly damaged, and he was not injured. Nonetheless, it was the worst day of his flying life to date. He was reprimanded by the Randolph brass, and worried that his days in the AT-6 might be over. But upon his return to Laughlin, his leadership proved to be in a forgiving mood, and no restrictions were placed on his flying.

The rest of spring 1945 was not eventful for Van. He continued to prepare to command the B-26 Marauder in combat. V-E Day, on 6 May, while long anticipated with the cessation of fighting in Europe weeks earlier, was a welcome release of tension. There was euphoric and well-deserved celebration at all US military facilities, including Laughlin Army Airfield.

In June, the changing war situation would throw another curve at Van's career progression. As fast as operations were drawing down in Europe, they were building up in the Pacific. Japan, although short on offensive victories of late, remained aggressively girding defenses in their main homeland islands. They were refusing all surrender proposals from the Allies. The US military was beginning to feel that a full-scale invasion might be the only way to end the war in the Pacific. Should such an offensive be necessary, it was decided that the longer range, higher bomb capacity, four-engine bombers would be the machines of choice, rather than the smaller twins such as the B-26.

Accordingly, many of the pilots in twin-engine transition training were reassigned to four-engine in the summer of 1945, including Van Shepard. So, despite having nearly completed his ground school and flying time in the Marauder at Laughlin, Van was ordered to report for transition on the B-24 Liberator heavy bomber at Liberal Army Airfield, Kansas. Here again, Van had mixed emotions about his situation. Yes, he wanted to go where he could be of greatest use to the war effort. Yes, here was an even larger ship, one of the largest, that would be at his command. But it also represented a starting-over of sorts. Given that the transition schools were continuing to have their durations lengthened, he would now be a "student" for much longer than he ever imagined. But in the end, as always, he faced his lot stoically, and left Laughlin on 25 June 1945 for a two week furlough in Monroe prior to reporting to Liberal.

As he had six months earlier, Van enjoyed reestablishing family, friend, and love relationships during his furlough. He decided to cut his furlough short two days, as he had the opportunity to fly from Barksdale Army Airfield near Shreveport to Randolph, and then to Wichita, Kansas, rather than going by train as was customary. After spending the night in a hotel in Wichita, he bused west to Liberal, arriving Saturday, 8 July 1945.

His entry into training on the B-24 went much as it had with the B-26 at Laughlin. The Consolidated B-24 Liberator was a high-wing four radial engine bomber, famous for its heroic deployments in the European theater. It ended up the most-produced bomber in US history, with over nineteen thousand built. The training aircraft at Liberal were almost all units returned from overseas with much combat experience; most were covered with dents, patches, and faded paint, making it hard for the pilots to conjure up enthusiasm for the coming activity. But they did their best. Heavy on the minds of each was the likelihood of a fall invasion of Japan; they knew they would be front and center if this occurred.

Then, a wildfire rumor spread through the base on the morning of 7 August that Japan had been hit with an atomic bomb. Hours later, President Harry Truman, in a radio address to the nation, confirmed that indeed Hiroshima had been destroyed the day before. The pilots began debating what this would mean for them. Then, another atomic bomb, this one targeting Nagasaki, was used on 9 August. Days later came the news that Japan was preparing for full capitulation, which came on Tuesday, 15 August 1945.

V-J Day. The second of two global celebrations. There would be no invasion of Japan. Van describes the somewhat subdued response at Liberal in this letter:

> That afternoon, Tue., at 6 pm, we heard that the war was over, and we thought we were going to celebrate. But what happened was that we had to fly; man, those instructors were mad because they had to fly. I didn't mind, for I still like to fly.
>
> Letter from Liberal Army Airfield, 18 August 1945

The next day, however, the reaction at the transition schools to the war's end was immediate. Until AAF leadership could establish longer term courses of action, most flying stopped. From Van, in the same letter:

> All flying and Ground School is stopped until further notice. We don't do anything but report for Roll Call at 0730 every morning. I have 64 hrs and was supposed to take my instrument check next time I go up, but it doesn't look like we will [fly] again.
>
> Letter from Liberal Army Airfield, 18 August 1945

Then, two days later, an interim schedule begins to take shape for the class:

> Tomorrow we start back on our ground school and Link [simulator]. We also go to the [flight] line, but I don't think it is to fly. Will let you all know all the "poop" from the "group" soon as I find out.
>
> Letter from Liberal Army Airfield, 20 August 1945

The fact is, the "poop" from the "group" turned out to be no more flying at Liberal. While post-war deployment strategies were being worked out, the pilots with college diplomas were moved into an on-site advanced academics program. Van embarked on a differential calculus course that had him soliciting his old math textbooks from home. In the meantime, several pilots with more service time were getting out altogether. With his lesser service, this was not an option that Van was considering.

On 7 September, the commander at Liberal received orders to inactivate the field by the end of the month. The B-24 transition school would be combined with others at Hondo Army Airfield in Texas, only ninety miles east of Van's old haunts at Laughlin. He and the other remaining pilots left Liberal on 19 September, practically "turning the lights out" behind them. Such was the nature of pilot training in post-war 1945.

The good thing about Van's subsequent time at Hondo was that he did get to resume his transition training. Both ground school and flight time proceeded, albeit at a more casual pace. The AAF was not anxious for its pilots to complete their training requirements while it was trying to consolidate its demobilization strategy. As at Laughlin, Van was also allowed to get hours in the AT-6, for which he was appreciative. Having experienced both the single- and multi-engine worlds now, he still had a definite preference for the smaller pursuit aircraft. He loved flying the Texan, and had learned to put on quite a show with it, often drawing spectators to the flight line when he was up in one.

He was also thinking a great deal about where he would go from here with his career. As had many pilots, Van had taken great interest in the latest aviation innovation, jet propulsion. He read everything he could find on the subject, and met one pilot passing through Hondo who had seen the Bell P-59 ("P" for Pursuit), America's first jet, fly at Muroc Army Airfield in California. Hoping to stack the deck in his favor, Van had begun diligent communication with his local leadership, and writing letters to others, on his desire for involvement with smaller aircraft, and jets in particular. In the meantime, he did become certified to command the Liberator in November, but received no orders to deploy with it. Furthermore, direction came down that Hondo Army Airfield was to be unceremoniously folded as well; all military personnel would be vacated before Christmas. He was issued a three-week furlough for the holidays, and told to await orders.

Van enjoyed the holidays at home. His brother Bill was also home, as a newly-promoted Aviation Radioman 3rd Class serving at Naval Air Station Jacksonville, Florida. The postwar dynamic was affecting Bill as well, as it was all servicemen. Though Van continued to encourage him toward pilot school, Bill had reservations now, and was contemplating alternatives of his own. The two young men helped each other balance their desires against what was available.

Van was not expecting to receive orders within the three week furlough. He resigned himself to having to play the waiting game. Then, between the holidays, came the wire that would change his life.

PART II

Test Pilot

Escalante, Utah, 7 March 1966, 9:46 am MST

As with all sophisticated aircraft, the XB-70 has redundancy built into its critical systems. For that reason, there are no less than four hydraulic supply systems on board, two for the flight control surfaces, and two for the utility systems such as landing gear and doors actuation. The B-70 was the first aircraft program to feature 4,000 pounds per square inch (psi) hydraulic pressure, instead of the usual 3,000, in order to save significant weight. However, with this technological leap came a host of development challenges, not the least of which was reliability. With both of the utility systems in failure, landing of the aircraft is at risk. Fortunately, most hydraulic system failure modes allow a minimal pressure to be sustained, so that critical functions such as landing gear extension can still be accomplished. Further, the Valkyrie also has an emergency electric gear extension feature that can be used to augment normal hydraulic deployment, but this feature had been troublesome in the past.

The pilots watched as pressure in the failed systems continued to drop. While he could continue to fly the plane safely enough, Shepard knew that they needed around 1,800 psi in one system to have a good chance at fully lowering the giant and complex main gear into place. Utility system #2 was already below 1,000 psi and still dropping; it was going to be useless. He held his breath as the utility system #1 gauge continued to drop towards that magic 1,800 number. While its rate of descent seemed to be slowing, it crept below 1,800.

"Stop . . ." he thought.

He reached down and felt for one of the yellow and black striped ejection system actuation handles. The Valkyrie's rocket-powered escape system had passed a rigorous test program, but had never been used in service. He then reminded himself that he needed to keep flying the airplane first and foremost; two lives were depending on this. He returned his focus to his flight instruments. That beautiful bird -- it was flying true as ever. Cotton asked how the controls felt; he noted that they felt normal. Of course, the flight controls operated off the separate primary hydraulic systems.

About that time Cotton convinced himself that the U1 needle was ending its descent. Sure enough, it was stabilizing at about 1,600 psi, but, in a sense, that was the worst place it could stop: higher, and they had a good shot with the gear; lower, and they could begin to execute a bailout plan. At 1,600, they were in the twilight zone. Cotton fed the news to the other men in the air and on the ground.

They had now slowed to Mach 1.1 (about 750 miles per hour) and 31,000 feet, with a good vector toward Edwards. As Air Vehicle #1 continued to decelerate, the TB-58A chase was approaching from the rear.

Al White radioed, "Zero-Zero-One, coming in from five o'clock. Gonna look you over real good."

The Hustler was maneuvered slowly around the larger craft, keeping a respectful distance from both the plane and its huge wake.

White called out, "No trace of fluid; nothing out of the

ordinary at all."

Shepard and Cotton were not sure whether this was good news or bad, but it was sure good to have company up there.

During the next several minutes, as the Valkyrie further decelerated, the men exchanged data and discussed various scenarios of action. Shepard did his best to concentrate on flying the airplane. There continued to be nothing amiss on the exterior reported by the Hustler. By this time they were 180 miles uprange of Edwards, at 270 miles per hour and 10,000 feet. Normal functionality in the primary hydraulics enabled Shepard to place the Valkyrie in her landing configuration: folding wingtips in their up position, for greatest lift; and windshield fairing in its down position, affording greatest visibility. Another chase plane, an F-104 Starfighter, joined the flight. Lieutenant Colonel Fitz Fulton, yet another XB-70 program pilot, was in the back seat. Shepard knew that crunch time was imminent.

Sure enough, ground communication called out, "OK, Joe, let's try the gear."

Cotton looked at his pilot, who nodded his readiness, and replied, "Roger, here we go."

He pushed down on the lever to extend the landing gear. It was always difficult to feel anything upon gear extension on the XB-70, given that its pilots rode 65 feet forward of the nose gear ("nose gear" being a misnomer in the case of the Valkyrie, but used nonetheless by tradition). The chase pilots watched the gear doors open and the gear begin to deploy, painfully slowly with the reduced hydraulic pressure. Cotton and Shepard watched for the green "gear down" lights with nervous anticipation. Nothing. Not one of the three gearsets succeeded in fully deploying.

Cotton called out, "OK, we've got no green lights, repeat, zero green."

"Roger that, One."

THE TIPTOEING VALKYRIE

Gazing up from the F-104, Fulton called out, "Yeah, we got problems with all three . . . "

*　　　　*　　　　*

SIX

Muroc

With P-80 Shooting Star, 1947

V AN COULDN'T BELIEVE HIS eyes: yes, the telegram said to report on 3 January 1946 to Muroc Army Airfield, California, for duty supporting flight test of experimental aircraft with the Air Technical Service Command. Somebody in Washington was listening! And here he had been thinking he'd end up flying cargo between North Dakota and Kansas, or something similar.

But there came with the same communique a piece of bad news, if not unexpected: Van was being classified as Active Air Forces

Reserve, no longer in the "Regular" Army Air Forces. This same reclassification was being applied to most new officer-pilots; it was more a reflection of the postwar demobilization than on Van's ability as a pilot. He would carry the same Second Lieutenant rank and pay. He packed his bags on New Year's Day, again said his goodbyes, and took the long train ride west.

Muroc had been around a long time, but had come to prominence during the war. About eighty miles north of Los Angeles, it was the new "proving ground of choice" for America's first jet aircraft; both the Bell P-59 Airacomet and the Lockheed P-80 Shooting Star were undergoing tests as Van arrived. Muroc's most unique feature was the dry lakebed of Rogers Lake, which provided up to eight miles of wide open hard-surface landing area for experimental aircraft that either needed a lot of room to land, or were in trouble. Only after the occasional heavy winter rains was the lakebed not available for use. The base also had conventional concrete runways for normal takeoff and landing use. On top of this, the area usually had perfect flying weather. It was aviation heaven-on-earth.

The morning after his arrival, Van was able to witness the takeoff of a Shooting Star. Its screaming turbojet was the most exciting sound he had ever heard. He couldn't wait for the day he might get in one.

After the usual check-in rituals, Van learned how he would start his Muroc tenure. As low man on the totem pole, and without combat experience, he would have to expect many of the least desirable pilot assignments. Indeed, he would do lots of "aerial errand running" and make many aircraft ferry trips in the first months of 1946. However, he also was granted liberal proficiency flying time, and spent many hours in his old buddy, the AT-6 Texan. Here at the centroid of the flying universe, though, his acrobatic skill did not garner as much attention as it did at Hondo.

He also checked out in two utility/cargo planes, the Beechcraft

UC-45 Expeditor and the Douglas C-47 Skytrain. The latter, derived from the venerable DC-3 airliner, was affectionately known as the "Gooney Bird". These aircraft he would use extensively for the aforementioned miscellaneous errands.

But he also was able to meet several front line test pilots, a few of whom would become famous in the annals of aviation. And with time, he was given assignments supporting the extensive test program underway on a brand new design: the Republic XP-84 Thunderjet. The "X" designating Experimental, this fighter (as the pursuit planes began to be called) was similar to the P-80, but featured a new axial-flow turbojet with even greater performance potential. One drawback of the Thunderjet was its high takeoff speed, some 160 mph; Van was amused at the predictable nickname of "World's Fastest Tricycle", due to takeoff runs that seemed to take forever.

The first prototype XP-84 made its maiden flight at Muroc on 28 February 1946. After a series of contractor tests, it was handed over to the Army in the summer for its own performance testing. Van had the privilege of attending meetings, flight debriefs, and company lectures associated with this testing, which enabled him to quickly expand his knowledge of jet propulsion. He would occasionally pilot photographic planes for the XP-84 test flights. How he loved watching it from alongside, and, even more, when it roared past him at more than double his speed.

Finally came the opportunity he was waiting for. As its testing on the P-59 wound down, the AAF decided to avail the thirty -B models as jet propulsion familiarization aircraft, first for the pilots at Muroc, and then elsewhere. After two weeks of ground school, Van took off on his first jet aircraft ride.

The Airacomet was not an outstanding performer, despite having twin turbojet engines. Both its airframe and its engines were a bit underachieving, understandable in that both represented first efforts for American aviation. In all respects, its performance was short of that of the piston engine P-51D Mustang, our top-performing pursuit plane at war's end. Nonetheless, it was robust and airworthy, and well suited to this indoctrination purpose.

Van Shepard didn't mind its performance limitations one bit. He loved the "fluid" feel of the jet, against the "pounding" feel of the piston powered aircraft. Even though the familiarization program imposed a 300 knot (about 350 miles per hour) speed limit, this was still a good 70 mph faster than Van had ever flown an airplane. He found it easy to fly and land, and was able to make two short flights in it.

The 25th of June 1946 was an exciting day at Muroc. The flight line was crowded with onlookers, including Van, as the Northrop XB-35 "Flying Wing" bomber made its maiden flight, from the Northrop plant in Hawthorne, California into Muroc. This innovative aircraft was just what its nickname implied: it had no separate fuse-lage or empennage (the term for the horizontal and vertical stabilizers at the tail). All of its capacity and its control surfaces were integrated into one large wing, with what was, at the time, one of larger wingspans ever flown at 172 feet. And it featured four of the largest piston engines in US aviation history, each powering dual counter-rotating propellers aft of the wing. It would remain a sight to behold in the months ahead, as it was put through its development paces.

About this time Van read in a letter from home that his brother Bill had decided not to become a pilot. He discharged from the Navy on 6 July 1946, and was enrolling for the fall term in the Electrical Engineering program at LSU. While Van was somewhat sad, he knew that Bill would make good on whatever path he took.

This realization caused Van to again be thinking about his own career path. He had developed a rapport with test pilot Wally Lien, who had made the XP-84's maiden flight, and was pilot on some of the flights that Van was supporting. Lien would listen to Van describe his aspirations to be in his position someday. He told Van that he had all of the flying skills and instincts he needed at this point in his career, but was lacking two feathers in his cap: he needed an engineering degree, and he needed flying squadron experience. Without these, it would be hard for him to reach his goals.

Van was not happy to hear this, but not surprised either. He began to think about how and when he might get back to school. What intrigued him was the Army Air Forces Institute of Technology, at Wright Field near Dayton, Ohio. An appointment to "AFIT" for engineering study had several advantages over enrolling in a public university: he would not have to discharge from the AAF, come up with tuition or a scholarship, find housing, etc. As he prepared to apply, he unfortunately learned that the rank of First Lieutenant or higher was required to enroll in the Engineering Sciences program at AFIT. Van did not think that a promotion to "1LT" was going to come soon, and began to have doubts once again about his career in the AAF.

He received a pick-me-up in August 1946, which put his career concerns on the back burner. A new program came to Muroc that would ensure that the base remained at the forefront of aviation technology: the Bell XS-1 rocket plane. This aircraft, while small and conventionally shaped, was designed from the beginning to exceed the speed of sound. The "XS" designation meant "experimental supersonic" (the XS-1 name was later shortened to X-1). It was powered by a four-chamber liquid propellant rocket engine. The plane was carried aloft by a modified B-29 bomber, and drop-launched before igniting its engine and starting its high speed flight. It then made an unpowered landing on the lakebed at Muroc. At the outset, Van was assigned to provide the same type of miscellaneous support to the program that he did for the XP-84, and relished the opportunity. After a series of glide flights, its first powered flight took place on 10 December.

Later came what he had been hoping for: he was designated a backup chase plane pilot for the XS-1 test flights. Thus, should anything prevent a primary chase pilot from flying, Van would suit up and pilot that chase plane for the test. Due to the high speed of the rocket plane, the fastest aircraft in AAF inventory were needed to serve as chase planes, namely the P-80. Van thus checked out in the production P-80A, the plane he had been watching fly since his first full day at Muroc a year earlier. He made his first flight in early 1947, but was never called on to fly chase for the XS-1.

Van continued his support of the XP-84 and XS-1 programs well into 1947. He was also able to continue his proficiency flying, mostly in the AT-6. Of course, he continued to draw the occasional "gopher" assignment as well. He described one such mission in a letter to home:

> Last Saturday I flew to Blythe, Calif to pick up a dismantled stor-
> age freezer. I had that C-47 up to max weight, 31,000 lbs, for
> takeoff, and it must have taken me 5 min to get climbing air
> speed. That old airplane just staggered off the runway.
>
> Letter from Muroc Army Airfield, 4 March 1947

From flying the fastest production jet in the US one day, to hauling a freezer in a beat-up Gooney Bird the next? Only in the Army Air Forces!

On the personal side, Van was beginning to allow himself the pleasure of developing more meaningful dating relationships, now that, for the first time, he was based at a facility he knew he would remain at for more than a few months. Being in the military (which still carried great weight in the postwar days), and, further, being the handsome officer-pilot, he seldom had to deal with the stress most men do in searching out suitable female companionship. It was more a matter of "which one today". A few of these love interests indeed developed into longer term relationships during his time at Muroc. However, what he really wanted was to combine his dating with his passion for aviation, in which he was not completely successful. Witness his description of one date, later in same letter:

> Oh yes, I flew a Taylorcraft in Bakersfield, Calif a couple weekends ago. I took one of my girlfriends up, and I couldn't even make a turn without her screaming and climbing all over me. Never again do I take these girls airplane riding.
>
> Letter from Muroc Army Airfield, 4 March 1947

In the spring of 1947 Van would get the fortuitous opportunity to check out in two very different aircraft, the first of them downright exotic. In order to ensure a wide breadth of flying experiences on the part of its Muroc pilots, the AAF had decided to have them fly the Northrop N-9M, a scaled-down version of the flying wing. The N-9M, flown at Muroc since 1943, featured a 60 foot wingspan, compared to the full scale version's 172 feet, and was powered by two small piston engines. Van got his turn, completed his short familiarization flight, and would

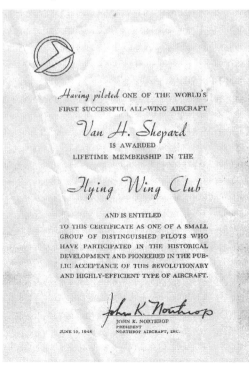

Having piloted ONE OF THE WORLD'S FIRST SUCCESSFUL ALL-WING AIRCRAFT

Van H. Shepard

IS AWARDED

LIFETIME MEMBERSHIP IN THE

Flying Wing Club

AND IS ENTITLED

TO THIS CERTIFICATE AS ONE OF A SMALL GROUP OF DISTINGUISHED PILOTS WHO HAVE PARTICIPATED IN THE HISTORICAL DEVELOPMENT AND PIONEERED IN THE PUBLIC ACCEPTANCE OF THIS REVOLUTIONARY AND HIGHLY-EFFICIENT TYPE OF AIRCRAFT.

John K. Northrop

JOHN K. NORTHROP
PRESIDENT
NORTHROP AIRCRAFT, INC.

JUNE 10, 1948

refer to it thereafter as "the empennageless wonder". He would be given a nifty certificate a year later, signed by "Jack" Northrop himself, declaring his membership in the "Flying Wing Club".

The second new ride for Van was in the Douglas A-26 Invader. The "A" designator meant Attack, and this represented his first chance to experience this type of aircraft. Following checkout, he ferried one 85 miles from Muroc to Naval Air Station Point Mugu, California. The Navy was assuming ownership of the plane, planning to convert it to a target towing aircraft as the JD-1. It was Van's first flight into a naval facility, and he enjoyed this interlude to his regular assignments.

Throughout these very different flying assignments at Muroc, Van continued to impress his leadership. He noticed that not all of the new pilots were being given the same opportunities as he for desirable assignments. In April, he was asked to fly a P-80A in a demonstration for a group of visiting federal legislators. The event was chronicled in the following article in his hometown newspaper:

> Members of the Wolverton congressional committee on Air Safety, while visiting Muroc flight test base in the Mojave desert in California, were given a flying demonstration by First Lt. Van H. Shepard, piloting a sleek new P-80 jet fighter. The demonstration was staged while the committee was being conducted on a tour of the base. Upon sight of the P-80 streaking across the field at a speed nearing 600 mph, all eyes were upward to witness Lt. Shepard execute a 9G pull-up from ground level, and zoom almost straight up to an altitude of eleven thousand feet.
>
> article in Monroe Morning World, April 1947

There was an error in this account: Van Shepard remained a Second, not First, Lieutenant, throughout his Muroc time. Further, the characterization of his speed as "nearing 600 mph" also may have been a bit charitable, for a production P-80A flying a demonstration. Nonetheless, this was another important and highly visible assignment completed by Van.

By now, Van had been at Muroc for seventeen months. He had seen a lot, and grown a lot, in his aviation career, far more than he could have imagined as he left his last assignment. It had been a great ride, but he was again beginning to think about where he might go from here. He still wanted to attend AFIT for his engineering degree, but he could not even apply until he received his promotion to First Lieutenant. He decided to await the promotion, then reassess his options. He hoped it would not be long in coming, as he had enjoyed some high-exposure successes, and had generally kept his record clean. Further, some great things were coming up at Muroc: the X-1 (as it was now called) resuming its push toward the sound barrier, a jet-powered version of the Flying Wing, a possible speed record attempt by the P-80, and there were rumors of an even faster jet fighter, all coming soon for testing. With his broadening resume, he would be sure to get some great assignments among these programs.

Then, as so often happens in the military, an altogether different situation presented itself. The AAF was looking for pilots in the Pacific. The postwar occupation of Japan was serious business: there was much work being done between the US and Japan in the establishment of a new normalcy in the region, hopefully to the benefit of both countries. The military's presence in this process was critical: there was burgeoning military air traffic of all sorts in and around Japan, and strong AAF presence was needed in order to manage it. Van Shepard was asked to take an assignment with a flying squadron in the western Pacific; the duration: 30 to 36 months.

At first, Van despised the very notion. He briefly considered leaving the AAF at one point. But then he remembered Wally Lien's suggestion that with a squadron assignment to complete his pilot's resume, he could later become a viable candidate for the best flight test assignments. And an assignment overseas would be yet another "box checked". He decided to take the opportunity, with two provisos: that his promotion to First Lieutenant would be a part of the deal, and that he would be assigned to a squadron that would operate jet fighters. These were agreed to, and he was slated to depart San Francisco in July 1947 for Japan.

Van left Muroc on 16 June for another three week furlough. He arrived back in Monroe to find many changes over the past year and a half. The biggest was the new store: "H. F." (as Huber had become known) and Marie were into an ambitious project to build a modern brick store to replace the original wooden structure. The new store

The new Shepard's under construction, 1947 (old store to the right)

was being built adjacent to, and east of, the old store, so that the latter could remain open during construction. To make room for the new building, they had moved the house about a hundred feet south, turning it ninety degrees to face McGuire Avenue instead of DeSiard Street.

Everyone in the family was excited about the changes. Bill was home from LSU, and sore from his summer job digging ditches. Sam and Frances were working in the store, having finished the tenth and ninth grades respectively. Both would attend Neville High School an extra year over what Van and Bill did, a twelfth grade having been newly added. Sam was enjoying playing American Legion baseball. Shepard's had hired a manager, Parker McGee, mostly to manage the service station. Parker proved to be just as valuable and loyal as Fred McCollum was, and would remain with them many years. The Shepards were well positioned for the postwar economic boom.

Selman Field, however, had undergone profound changes of the opposite sort since war's end. Navigation training had ended almost immediately, with those students remaining in the program transferred to Texas. For a time, the base was used as a separation center for discharging Army personnel. Now, it was practically a ghost town. The city of Monroe operated the small commercial airport there, and crop dusting once again anchored general aviation use. Van nostalgically drove around the grounds one afternoon, seeing row after row of abandoned barracks sitting where the old runways used to be. It was a bittersweet experience.

As always, Van used his furlough to reconnect with friends that were still in Monroe, particularly female. One of the women he had dated on his Christmas 1945 furlough, Freda Clifton, was still around. Originally from Shreveport, she and Van got back together, and began seeing each other daily. Van began to wish he wasn't about to head overseas, for he enjoyed Freda more than any of his California girlfriends. The two promised each other they would stay in close contact by mail, and Van hoped this meant that she might still be around when he returned stateside. Right after the fourth of July, he said his goodbyes and boarded a train for San Francisco.

Van went to Hamilton Army Airfield, on the north end of San Francisco Bay, to stage his 12 July departure for Japan. Hamilton was used as the primary transshipment port for Army personnel moving into or out of the Pacific theater. He had several preparatory tasks to complete, this being his first overseas deployment. While awaiting his departure, he also had the opportunity to take on miscellaneous assignments for the squadrons at Hamilton. One was to copilot a B-25J to Los Angeles and back on the 11th. He enjoyed seeing the familiar terrain around Muroc, just a few miles east of his flight plan. He wondered if he would ever see it again.

SEVEN

Okinawa

O N 12 JULY 1947, Van Shepard boarded the US Army Transport *General C. G. Morton* and began the long sea voyage to Japan. There were multiple stopovers. The most enjoyable for him was Honolulu; he spent most of three days there. The following note was written from the ship a few days after leaving Honolulu:

> I had a pretty good time in Honolulu. Went out to the Royal Hawaiian Hotel which is right down on Waikiki Beach. It was the most beautiful hotel I have ever seen. Irving Berlin and daughter were visiting Hawaii. I saw them at the hotel. We left Honolulu 1500 [hours] 22 July 47 and I saw Pearl Harbor off our

starboard side, as we were leaving Honolulu Harbor.

Letter from the *Morton* on the western Pacific, 27 July 1947

Later in the same letter, an interesting excerpt on one of any world voyager's more significant accomplishments:

. . . yesterday at 1635 [hours] our position was 180°00'00" Longitude, 20°54'00" Latitude, which was the time we crossed the international date line. Just before we crossed the line, the time in Monroe was 2235 (25 July) but just after we crossed this line we gained twenty-four hours (to 26 July) on you people. Now we are eighteen hours ahead of you instead of being six hours behind.

Everyone aboard joined the Domain of the Golden Dragon (the ruler of the 180th meridian).

Letter from the *Morton* on the western Pacific, 27 July 1947

The voyage proved to be relatively weather-free; only one benign front passed over during the twenty-five days at sea. Taking advantage of the clear weather, the dark night skies, and time on his hands, Van managed to further his knowledge of astronomy during the trip.

The *Morton* docked at Yokohama harbor on 5 August 1947. The officers went by train to a personnel depot in the town of Haramachida, 27 miles to the west. Prior to armistice, the facility was a Japanese military academy. The men were housed 36 to a barracks; Van would remark that it was like being in boot camp again. After the usual physicals, forms filling, etc., the men awaited their destinies: there were air bases in need of staffing not only in the main four Japanese islands, but in Okinawa, Guam, Philippines, and Korea as well. Placement would depend on matching the men's Military Occupational Specialties (M.O.S.) with needs at each base. After a few days, Van learned that his destination would be Naha Air Base, on the island of Okinawa, and that his first position would include aircraft maintenance responsibility. He transferred there in late August.

There were two main AAF air bases on Okinawa, at Naha and Kadena, plus several smaller airfields elsewhere. Okinawa is about six miles by sixty-five miles, and is located one thousand miles southwest of Tokyo. Being at the same latitude as Miami, the climate is tropical. But Van found that life was going to be difficult at Naha: not only were basic personal goods hard to come by, but his fleet of airplanes were in dire need of maintenance parts. As he noted in his first letter from the base:

> Dad, I finally got settled down in my job. We are really having great troubles getting parts and supplies for our airplanes. The island just doesn't get enough supplies from the depots in Guam and Japan. You can't get air shipments on parts unless the airplane is out of commission, therefore you just don't get parts until you order parts for a grounded airplane, even though a normal requisition for the parts has been in for several months. This situation keeps about half of our airplanes grounded all the time.
>
> Letter from Naha Air Base, 8 September 1947

While Van felt he would gain valuable experience on the "nuts & bolts" side of the aviation business in this assignment, which would serve him well later in his career, he would have to show a great deal of patience with the supply situation, as the remote military infrastructure caught up with his needs.

What did concern him at this time was his inability to fly. He had not flown an airplane since he left Hamilton, the longest such drought in his career. He knew that flying was not going to be his primary focus with his maintenance assignment, but he had hoped he would be able to do proficiency flying in the base's AT-6 Texans. But with the parts problems the base was having, this was not going to happen. So Van had some additional, more personal incentive to help get the parts situation resolved. In September, he did at least have the opportunity to copilot a Curtiss C-46 Commando to the nearby island of Ie Shima, carrying parts for a needy pursuit plane.

There were two significant pieces of news that Naha received later in 1947. First, on 18 September, it was announced that the long-awaited establishment of the United States Air Force as a separate service had taken effect. Among the officer-pilots, at first there was optimism that this could serve to enhance their careers. But in time, as additional details were released, some of this optimism waned. For example, the rank structure would be the same as it was in the AAF, as would the pay grades. A USAF-specific uniform had not even been designed yet. Soon enough, it would be back to business as usual in Okinawa.

The second piece of news, coming from Muroc, was of great personal satisfaction to Van Shepard. His old program, the Bell X-1, had succeeded in breaking the sound barrier at the hands of test pilot Captain Chuck Yeager, on 14 October 1947. It was perhaps fitting that this happened less that a month after the establishment of the independent USAF. How Van would have loved to have been there – he wondered who got the chase plane assignments. The reports indicated that there appeared to be no substance to the concern that there might be some sort of physical "barrier" or control difficulty upon passing through "Mach One", good news indeed. Van took pride in the fact that he himself had already touched Mach 0.8, in the P-80A. He was confident that he, too, was going to accomplish this feat someday.

At this time, things would be looking up for Van getting back into flying. First and foremost, the parts supply situation was improving. The base had a visit from the western Pacific commanding general, who, as he was leaving, committed to putting some heat on the parts situation. Second, the USAF was finally recognizing the need to maintain the proficiency of its pilots in non-flying assignments. It formed the 18th Airdrome Squadron, consisting of "Wing Flight Sections" for the express purpose of providing proficiency flying for pilots in maintenance and operations positions. Van was thus able to get back in the air regularly, logging twenty-two hours in October.

On the domestic front, his roommate at Naha was another officer-pilot named John Ambrecht, who was married and anticipating the arrival of his wife and two young children in the coming summer. In the meantime, Van and John shared an apartment and employed a young Okinawan housekeeper named Yashi'ko.

In November, Van went through his first episode of what was a common challenge for many USAF bases in the western Pacific: a typhoon alert. He detailed his experience in the following letter:

> The other night, I was notified by the weather office that we (Okinawa) were in a Typhoon Alert Area, and that the winds were expected up to 55 miles per hour by morning. Since the Engineering Officer was in Manila, I had to get the men together so that we could get the AT-6's ready. What I mean by ready is that the airplanes have to be headed into the wind, and we place six sandbags on each wing, four on the tail, and three on each wheel. The airplanes are parked on a coral ramp, so we have no provisions for tying them down. By 2300, we had the aircraft turned and sand-bagged.
>
> After all the precautions, the typhoon was diverted off to the east by high pressure moving in this area. Can't take any chances.
>
> Letter from Naha Air Base, 13 November 1947

The island would be placed on typhoon alert on at least two other occasions during the 1947 storm season. One storm, Typhoon Flora, hammered Naha with 65 mph sustained winds, but did little damage.

The men received a day and a half off for Christmas. The high-light of the holiday was a dance party and dinner, visited by the Brigadier General over all of the bases on Okinawa, and his wife. And with the new year came some good news: that promotion to First Lieutenant that Van was promised came through, with its attendant increase in pay. He also picked up the additional responsibility of Squadron Supply Officer, in charge of requisitioning material for his squadron, not just airplane parts, but everything down to office supplies.

Settling into 1948, the pilots were getting more hours of proficiency flying, mainly in the T-6 (the Air Force dropped the "A" from the Texan's designation). While he was happy to get more hours in the Texan, he looked forward with great anticipation to the arrival of the P-80 for squadron duty in Okinawa. He attended maintenance school on the Shooting Star in preparation.

For a time, Van was intrigued by the possibility of flying for "Civil Air Transport", the airline newly launched by now Major General Chennault in China. The airline provided supplies and food relief support to war-ravaged China and Chiang Kai-shek's Nationalists. Many of the airline's first pilots were former AAF Pacific theater pilots. But Van decided to continue in the Air Force, hoping that his time in Okinawa would indeed lead to something special in the future.

Continuing its rebound from World War II, commercial air transport was beginning to proliferate in the western Pacific. Okinawa figured heavily in this: before the war, the Naha facility was the commercial airport for the nearby city of the same name, which is also the seat of Okinawa prefecture. It is strategically located as a refueling stop between the large northern cities and the Philippines or Guam. Commercial air travel now having been restored, the USAF base was sharing the field with the airport; this was common for many bases in the Pacific. Indeed, multiple airlines scheduled commercial flights into and out of Naha daily.

Local air traffic control for both military and civil flights remained the responsibility of the USAF. As part of his many different officer responsibilities, Van Shepard would occasionally take shifts as Airdrome Officer, overseeing air traffic control operations at Naha. Thus his time in Okinawa was providing him with yet another aviation-related experience that he was unlikely to get stateside.

Beginning in February 1948, a series of events transpired which had him on a roller coaster of emotions. They are best described by Van himself, in their entirety in the following letter to his family:

Dear Folks,

I know you people have waited a long time for a letter, for I have not written in about a month or more. I sure have intended to write, but I was just plain tired or upset.

To begin back in Feb., where I left off, I have been transferred from the Service Group to the First Fighter Group, 25th Fighter Sqdn. This transfer came about because as of 29 Feb 1948 I was placed on a competitive tour of duty to determine if I am capable of holding a Regular commission. As you know, I am in the Active Air Force Reserve and this tour will determine if I get Regular or not. To serve this tour, I had to be assigned to a flying unit therefore I was transferred, and this action made me very happy. I am now flying P-80's learning to be a fighter pilot, and as expected I am having a little difficulty, for I have no fighter time and my sense of flying has been experienced in twin and four engine type aircraft or in other words a "Bomber pilot". Now I have to learn all over, even though I have 20 previous hours in the P-80. This time was flight test work and not fighter work.

I got checked out in the P-80 the other day, and I was very happy to get back to flying again after some 10 months of getting [only] 10 hrs a month. Then the trouble started. I was given a P-80 with tip tanks (1800 lbs more) to fly. (The first flight was made without tip tanks. I had made two previous tip tank rides at Muroc in March of '47.) I started my take-off roll and the airplane hit some rough bumps in the runway, and I became airborne prematurely in a nose high attitude. The airplane was stalling back into the runway because my airspeed was too slow, so I attempted to put the airplane back on the runway, but it bounced again and I then had drifted off the runway, so I jettisoned the tip tanks and one tank did not leave the wing; this pulled that wing down. (With one tip tank on you can't keep that wing up unless you have more than 130 mph.) I hit the ground hard and slid to a stop at the end and to the right side of the runway. The airplane was a complete wreck. My first accident in 1160 hours. This happened on the 10th of March. I wasn't hurt; not even a scratch.

The next day Freda notified me through a "Dear John" letter that she was marrying another boy. Of course that went just fine with me, like heck! But what else could I expect.

I have had two flights in the P-80 since the accident and I did O.K. The runway was the primary factor in my accident, but the accident board gave me 90% pilot error for letting the airplane drift off the runway and not putting it back on the runway and stopping it.

I have a good Sqdn. C.O., and he didn't get mad for tearing up one of his beautiful P-80's. My primary job now is a fighter pilot (jet) and I have an added duty of Ass't Eng. Officer.

Letter from Naha Air Base, 28 March 1948

Van rebounded fast from his misfortune, which was not held

against him going forward. He continued to accumulate extensive flying time in the P-80, including formation flying with a squadron of up to sixteen aircraft and 37,000 feet altitude in May. Later he was learning combat flying techniques, including weekly practice interception of B-29 bombers. He had accumulated eighty hours in the P-80 by mid-June.

Much to his dismay, he learned of the 5 June 1948 crash of the second YB-49 jet "Flying Wing" during testing out of Muroc, killing all five aboard. Having flown the N-9M "Little Wing" in 1947, this accident hit close to home for Van. He knew the copilot, Captain Glen Edwards, who also had flown the N-9M. Muroc would be renamed Edwards Air Force Base in Glen's honor eighteen months later.

That summer Van received that Regular Air Force commission he was seeking, together with one of the most coveted Military Occupational Specialty codes: no. 1059, Jet Fighter Pilot. While his P-80 flying performance made him deserving, he nonetheless felt fortunate to get it, as all of his transition training was on bombers. With this new designation, he was able to proceed into aerial gunnery with the P-80, in which he would shoot at towed targets. In one such test he scored 44 hits out of 200 rounds, which was considered excellent performance.

One issue that Van had to deal with in fighters that he would not have had to in bombers: his weight. Due to the fighters' smaller cockpit size, and they really were small, there was a largely unenforced 190 pound weight limit. Van would bounce around this number for most of the years he was flying fighters; it represented a nice incentive for him over the years to watch his weight.

Van began to make training missions to Japan's main island of Honshu with his squadron. One such trip in July lasted a full week, with landings at multiple American bases. A November mission took the squadron to Shanghai, his first visit to China.

In the meantime, Van learned of some significant changes in the life of his brother Bill. In order to hasten his graduation, Bill attended summer school in Baton Rouge, and had enough credits to receive his Bachelor of Science degree in Electrical Engineering in August 1948. Van was proud of his middle brother, the first to receive a four-year degree in the family. On top of that, Bill accepted an engineering position with the National Advisory Committee for Aeronautics (the predecessor of today's National Aeronautics and Space Administration), adjacent to Langley Air Force Base, Virginia (all "Army Air Fields" became "Air Force Bases" early in 1948). He moved to nearby Hampton, and started his job at the end of August.

Bill was not done making news. He and his girlfriend Mary Lois Stampley announced their engagement in October. After graduating from high school in Winnsboro, Louisiana in 1946, Lois had been working as a secretary at Sally Grocery Company's office in Monroe. The happy couple planned an April 1949 wedding.

Van's youngest brother was also making news back home. Sam had decided to complete the twelfth grade at Neville High, which was optional for his class, given the school was completing the process of adding the extra year. This turned out to pay great dividends for Neville's football squad: Sam was one of the quickest boys on the team that fall, and Van relished receiving news clippings chronicling his little brother's touchdowns.

Another piece of good news had arrived in the fall of 1948. Van found out that his overseas deployment would be reduced from thirty to twenty-four months total. Further, he would be returning to stateside duty in February after only eighteen months, and serve the remaining six months of the assignment with a squadron at Hamilton Field, or Hamilton Air Force Base as it was now called. But, prior to his departure, Mother Nature had a gift for Van for his twenty-fourth birthday: Typhoon Libby would strike Okinawa with a direct hit on 4 October 1948.

Libby had struck the island of Iwo Jima, eight hundred miles east of Okinawa, five days earlier. Despite its eye passing within seven miles of shore, generating wind gusts of up to 175 mph, there was no loss of life for American servicemen stationed there. The slow moving storm was headed in the direction of Okinawa, but forecasters noted that the eye was expected to pass well to the south of the island. Nonetheless, the airmen and officers prepared their facilities and aircraft, as they had with every such alert in the area.

The forecasters were wrong. Libby turned north on the afternoon of the 3rd, and hammered both Naha and Kadena all night long. Naha, the farther south of the two, sustained a maximum wind gust of 122 mph from the east. Then, just after dawn on the 4th, the eye of the storm passed directly overhead, providing a eerie calm lasting seven hours. This gave the men a chance to bolster their defenses against the other side of the storm they knew was coming. They reinforced the sandbagging of exposed aircraft, and turned them 180°, such that they would be favorable to the new wind direction.

As the back eyewall passed over that afternoon, winds up to 95 mph were recorded from the west. As at Iwo Jima, there was no loss of life at Okinawa, but Naha and Kadena together sustained an estimated $10,000,000 damage to buildings and aircraft. Thanks to the efforts of Van and his mates, there was little damage to their squadron's aircraft, just lots of coral bits to be purged from intakes. Only one F-80 (as P-80's were now called) was written off, taken out by a large piece of flying debris. The buildings, however, were another story. All of Naha's structures had significant damage. Van's quarters, while only taking two inches of water from the storm, nonetheless sustained major wind damage to both siding and roofing. Contractors would spend the rest of the year repairing damage to facilities at Naha. Van would never again want to see another tropical weather event.

Fortunately, given the minimal damage to its fleet, the 25th Fighter Squadron at Naha was able to continue with its flying and combat training, with little interruption. However, what free time they had was now spent in the cleanup operation and attempting to replace documentation lost to the storm. This would be the situation for the remainder of Van's time at Naha. There was little time off for the holidays, and the last four months would go by fast.

Van said goodbye to his airmen, his fellow officers, and their families, and shipped out aboard the US Army Transport *General F. W. Hase* on 24 February 1949. The eastbound journey to San Francisco followed an almost identical itinerary as the westbound one on the *General Morton,* albeit in reverse. The ship was even of the same Squier class of personnel transport.

He crossed back over the International Date Line, unceremoniously this time. He was amused by the thought that he had just "lost" that day he had "gained" eighteen months earlier, crossing in the other direction. As he had in his westbound trip, he spent two nights in Honolulu, well enjoyed and well deserved. The trip once again would require three and a half weeks in total.

Van never forgot that good counsel given him back at Muroc. Now he had in his pocket that fighter squadron experience, in an overseas jet squadron to boot; this was a formidable combination as far as Air Force career advancement potential goes. All the way home, he kept thinking about that other half of the suggestion: the engineering degree. His brother Bill's success at LSU did nothing but stoke his resolve. He still believed that the USAF Institute of Technology was his best plan, and as a First Lieutenant now, he was clear of the rank-related admission requirement. He would have to deal with this upon his arrival.

THE TIPTOEING VALKYRIE

The *General Hase* pulled under the Golden Gate Bridge on 21 March 1949, with all hands on deck to view the spectacle. She then made a turn to port, and headed on up to her debarkation dock at Van's new post, Hamilton AFB. It was so good to be home.

EIGHT

AFIT

In F-84 Thunderjet, ca 1951

URING HIS LAST FEW days at sea, Van received the squadron assignment that he would start upon his return to Hamilton. It was the best of news. He would join the 78th Fighter Group of the Air Defense Command, which had the responsibility for defense of the Pacific coast. He would be assigned to the 84th Fighter Squadron, something he was excited about: the 84th was transitioning from the P-51 Mustang to the F-84 Thunderjet, the latter from Van's old test program at Muroc! Hamilton was just now receiving its first deliveries of this high performance day fighter. Van couldn't wait to climb into that bird; he had so envied the more experienced pilots who got to test it in its infancy at Muroc.

Van requested, and was granted, a three-week furlough to begin following his repatriation. He had an extenuating circumstance as a reason: Bill had asked him to serve as his best man in his wedding.

Before leaving, Van made sure to collect a newly-released USAF officer's uniform, in the new blue color, to replace his well-worn AAF uniform. He wanted to stand up for Bill looking his snappiest. The new uniforms were hard to come by, as the Air Force was still using up stock of the old green AAF uniforms. Following a relaxing two weeks in Monroe, the wedding took place in Hampton, Virginia on 15 April 1949. Sam, Sis, and mother Marie were also able to attend; Huber stayed behind to mind Shepard's. Van returned to California the following day.

Van checked out in the F-84B soon after arriving back at Hamilton. While in Okinawa, he had heard of structural deficiencies in early production F-84's. The particular -B models at Hamilton had received upgrades to correct these structural deficiencies, so he was more confident of their airworthiness. His timing was perfect: the winter weather season had ended in the San Francisco Bay area. Most days were sunny in the northern end of the bay, but there was sometimes fog to deal with in morning takeoffs and landings. The "84th" (by fortunate coincidence, now sharing its ordinal designation with its primary aircraft) busied itself with daily patrols up and down the Pacific coast.

In the meantime, Van was acting on his AFIT plans. Fortunately, all of his background and transcript documentation survived the flooding in Typhoon Libby. Playing up all of his accomplishments and experience that he knew would be important, such as his Muroc time, his Okinawa time, his maintenance and air traffic control gigs, and last but not least, his MOS as a jet fighter pilot, he submitted his formal application for admission to AFIT for the fall term. He could now only play the waiting game, something every service man gets used to doing.

By July, the -D model of the F-84 was being delivered at Hamilton, which, in addition to being scratch-built with all the same structural upgrades that had been retrofitted to the -B, also featured a more powerful engine. Van was able to advance his personal speed record to 590 mph in his first week in the "dash-D". It was a great time: he was beginning to think that life would not be so bad after all, should he have to remain at Hamilton.

He got his answer from Dayton soon enough. Van Shepard was accepted at the United States Air Force Institute of Technology at Wright-Patterson Air Force Base, Ohio, for enrollment in the Engineering Sciences program! Classes would begin in September 1949. The Shepard family was proud of him: only eleven percent of those admitted to the E.S. program were Lieutenants; the others were Captains and higher, with even a Lieutenant Colonel in the class. Van would be rubbing elbows with some serious brass for the next two years.

The year 1949 would turn out to be a banner one for all the Shepard kids, insofar as education was concerned. Not only did Van enroll at AFIT and Bill graduate at LSU, but Sam graduated from Neville High and enrolled at Louisiana Tech in Ruston to study business, and Sis entered her senior year at Neville. All of the children were admirably accounting for themselves in their education.

Van finished up his squadron duty at Hamilton. On his last patrol, he admitted to having a few pangs of remorse as he cruised the clear blue skies in his Thunderjet. How he hoped his flight time wouldn't suffer too much at AFIT. He moved on to Dayton, and set up housekeeping in a room in an on-base dormitory for single student-officers.

Van found Dayton to be in a picturesque and interesting setting. It is situated on the Great Miami River, in the midst of the southern-most glacial moraines from the ice age. The city itself was industrial, with many General Motors auto parts plants, the headquarters of National Cash Register, and other large companies. It is only an hour or so from Cincinnati, which was of interest to Van with its General Electric jet engine design, test, and production facility at Evendale.

But Dayton's big attraction was aviation. No other city could boast of such dominance. It was home to the Wright Brothers, and the very field where they made their local development flights, Huffman Prairie, is wholly within the boundaries of today's sprawling Wright-Patterson Air Force Base, to the northeast of downtown. A splendid memorial to the Wrights was erected in 1940 on a hilltop contiguous with base property. The base also incorpo-rated both the AFIT campus and a small Air Force Technical Museum. Early on, Wright and Patterson Fields were separate facili-ties about five miles apart; they merged in 1945 to form WPAFB.

The origins of AFIT go back to 1919, when the first Air School of Application was created by the War Department. It was located at McCook Field, closer to what is now downtown Dayton, and moved to Wright Field in 1927. After closing during World War II, it was reestablished as an institute in 1947. Today it serves as the USAF's graduate school, with undergraduate education provided by the US Air Force Academy in Colorado Springs, Colorado. AFIT's adminis-tration and classroom facilities are clustered in a small campus located on the western or "Wright side" of WPAFB.

Also sited at WPAFB, on the "Patterson side", was the USAF Experimental Flight Test Pilot School. Van Shepard was interested in the school as a possible endeavor for himself someday, given his experiences at Muroc. Indeed, several of his former associates at Muroc would become graduates of the Test Pilot School, including Chuck Yeager. Van would closely follow activities there during his time at AFIT.

THE TIPTOEING VALKYRIE

On campus, the young pilot from Louisiana found himself just a bit overwhelmed early on. Seemingly, he was always in the company of some highly credentialed officers, even among his fellow students. As at Muroc, he once again felt like he was "low on the totem pole". Furthermore, academics was not Van's strongest suit: unlike his brother Bill, he would rarely excel in pure math and science in the classroom. As a result, he would struggle with his coursework at the outset. He came to realize that he would have to work harder than most in order to succeed, and took full advantage of tutoring and other forms of assistance available. Gradually, he began to assimilate, and with many a long night was able to deliver in his academic pursuits.

AFIT used the quarter system, with each of four annual terms lasting approximately eleven weeks. Compared to the traditional semester system, the quarter system had advantages and disadvantages: students took fewer courses each term, but each was more intensive, requiring more hours both in the classroom and studying. One did not have to stay focused as long in any one course, but if one fell behind, it was tough to recover in the short time available. Van managed to survive.

Albeit with little free time to experience it, he enjoyed campus life once again, after six years away from it. He made friends easily, joined the baseball league, and dated local women occasionally. Best of all, the pilots among the students, which were most of them, were provided the opportunity to maintain flying proficiency in aircraft within with their MOS. So Van was able to fly F-80's, and later, F-84's, out of Wright Field, within walking distance of campus. He found his flying to be therapeutic to his ability to manage the stress of his academics; he would return to his studies re-energized after a flight.

Early in 1950, Van was enrolled in a class studying weather in stratospheric flight. As innovative weather measurement techniques were under development at the National Advisory Committee for Aeronautics (NACA), in Virginia, AFIT made arrangements to have this class attend a two day seminar there on the subject. Of course, this was where Van's brother Bill had been working for over a year as an electrical engineer. Van looked forward to connecting with Bill and Lois during his visit. What is more, he found that NACA's instrumentation group was to give a presentation to the class on measurement of atmospheric wind gust velocity, and none other than Bill Shepard delivered the presentation! Both brothers were struck by the irony of younger brother Bill lecturing to older brother Van. The brothers and Lois, who was expecting her first child, had a great time at dinner that evening.

A few weeks later, Van received the happy news that he had indeed become an uncle: Bill and Lois were the proud parents of a boy, William Louis Jr. (the fourth male in the family to carry this name). As a gift, Van sent "Billy" a pillow, his very first.

Later that spring, back in Monroe, sister Frances graduated from Neville High; she would follow her brother Sam to Louisiana Tech in the fall.

The world political situation would once again change on 25 June 1950: the Soviet and Chinese supported North Korean military forces invaded South Korea. The United Nations Security Council, led by the United States, authorized immediate response, and a de facto, if undeclared, state of war once again existed for the US. Van Shepard was just starting his summer term at AFIT, nearing the halfway point toward his planned graduation.

An air war was initiated almost immediately. It represented the first time in which jet-powered fighters engaged in air-to-air combat. In the US arsenal were several F-80 and F-84 squadrons. For a time, Van Shepard believed it inevitable that he would be pulled out of AFIT and sent to combat. After all, he was fully current and combat-certified in both aircraft, and had squadron experience in Japan, from which many of the UN air missions were being launched. But the Air Force, to its credit, held fast to the premise that those officer-pilots in academic education be deployed to combat only in the most dire of war circumstances. The undeclared war in Korea was not deemed to be at that level. Furthermore, the war against the Communist forces was being waged by the United Nations, not directly by the United States. Most of the AFIT students were given the option to stay or leave for combat. A few did leave, but most elected to continue with their studies, and were able to complete them without interruption by the war.

Now, secure in the knowledge that he would be able to complete his studies, Van began eyeing the light at the end of the tunnel. He, and the Air Force, began to think about his next move after AFIT. Would he be sent to Korea? Back to Hamilton? Into flight instruction somewhere? Did he have a real shot at the Test Pilot School (which, incidentally, had just moved from "Wright-Patt" to Edwards AFB, as Muroc was now called)? Maybe something altogether different?

His strong preference was to become a test pilot. He made this known to his leadership, and submitted his application to Test Pilot School. But he would also be honor-bound to enter air combat were he called upon. He would trust that the Air Force would do what was necessary.

The answer that came down surprised him, once again. Van would join the Wright Air Development Center (WADC), right there at WPAFB, in Fighter Test Operations. As a WADC pilot, he would then be sent to Test Pilot School (TPS), but not immediately after graduation: there were insufficient openings at TPS, and he would have to await one.

What a great plan! He was as excited as he could be. He dove into his remaining studies at AFIT with renewed vigor, to ensure that he would do as well as possible. He knew that consummation of his path was predicated on successful graduation, and furthermore, he knew that Test Pilot School included a great deal of academic study of advanced aeronautics. The better he did in his remaining engineering coursework, the easier it would be to learn at TPS.

Van completed the requirements for his Bachelor's Degree in Engineering Sciences with his seventh term, in the spring of 1951. His graduation took place on Thursday, 7 June. Van was one of only five Lieutenants graduating in the E.S. program. In attendance at the commencement ceremony, all the way from Louisiana, was proud mother Marie. She was thrilled to be able to make the trip, not only to see Van graduate, but she was born and raised in Edgerton, Ohio, about 150 miles north of Dayton. After the ceremony, she and Van took the opportunity to drive to Edgerton for a short visit with cousins still in town. It was the only time Van would visit there; he enjoyed seeing the still-standing home, church, and school of his mother when she was a girl, as well as the graves of many ancestors in the local cemetery. He was impressed with a stained glass window dedicated to his great-great-grandparents, Adam and Elizabeth Weitz, in the Methodist church where his mother's family had worshiped.

NINE

Test Pilot School

Unofficial Test Pilot School logo

V AN SHEPARD ENTHUSIASTICALLY STARTED his assignment at Wright-Patt's 2750th Air Base Wing, supporting the Wright Air Development Center, on 24 June 1951. The WADC operated an extensive collection of facilities adjacent to Wright Field. It was responsible for all manner of evaluation and testing of everything related to aircraft, not only through flight testing, but in disciplines such as aerodynamic drag, aircraft engine fuels, weapons systems, and materials. Among its flight specializations were all-weather flying, in-flight refueling, and evaluation of captured or politically defected enemy aircraft. Van entered his tenure at WADC as an engineering pilot; he would fly specially equipped production aircraft on which systems, components, or instruments from an experimental program were evaluated in the flight environment. He would thus gain valuable exposure to many facets of aviation research and development, while awaiting his slot at Test Pilot School.

Van received a long-awaited promotion to Captain in September 1951. He had anticipated this happening in conjunction with his graduation back in June, but of course was happy to take it a bit later.

Around the Christmas holidays, he was notified that an opening was available at the USAF Experimental Flight Test Pilot School at Edwards. He prepared to leave Dayton, move to Edwards, and enroll. He was excited about his plan to become a certified test pilot.

In January 1952, for the third time, he headed to California, this time back to the Mojave Desert. He found Edwards Air Force Base to be quite different from the Muroc Army Airfield he left four and a half years earlier, due to changes wrought by time and the war. The new-found attention garnered by the testing of the new jets and X-planes had enabled expansion in many areas: there were new build-ings everywhere. But he found quite a few friends still around, and overall it was great to be back.

Van would again be housed in an on-base dormitory for single officers, not far from the quarters where he was posted in 1946-47. He would share a wing with his fellow classmates at TPS. As the first class commencing in 1952, his class was designated "52-A", in the same manner that regular pilot school classes were. His classmates included six other US Air Force officers, a Royal Canadian Air Force officer, and an aircraft company pilot. Instruction to the nine students in 52-A began on 28 January.

The Test Pilot School had just been reorganized as it was moved to Edwards from Wright-Patt. Military aviation was undergoing rapid innovation at the time, with many technological advances in the works. The Air Force was keen on ensuring that it would have enough test pilots, with the right skills, to manage its future development programs. It thus placed great priority on the TPS, as its means of creating this needed expertise. The TPS was structured much like any college graduate school: it had a faculty, courses organized by topic and level, and credit hours assigned to each course according to the time commitment involved. There were usually three classes graduated each year. Class duration was about seven months; thus each class would overlap with others in progress.

The instruction was rigorous. It included academic study in aerodynamics and related aeronautical engineering subjects, as well as practical test flying in aircraft of known flight characteristics. Also taught were the use of techniques required in testing experimental aircraft, reduction of data obtained in the fields of performance and stability & control, and writing test reports. The aircraft used for instruction were specially equipped B-25's, F-80's, and T-28's. The latter, the North American T-28 Trojan, was new to Van, but he was very familiar with the similar aircraft it replaced, the T-6 Texan.

Instruction was served up in three phases. The short first phase consisted of refreshers in various math and physics topics, with no flying. The second involved theory and practice of performance flight testing. The final phase covered theory and practice of stability & control flight testing. Each student flew his own tests, reduced the data gathered in the flight, and analyzed the results. The student then submitted a report of all data, his analysis, and his conclusions. A new daily schedule was implemented with Van's class, wherein the mornings were devoted to flying and data reduction, and the afternoons to four 50-minute lectures. Those students graduating will have completed 114 academic credit hours, plus 123 total hours of flight time (85 in the performance phase and 58 in the stability & control phase).

The classes also received a tour of one or more nearby aircraft manufacturer facilities, which included lectures by company engineers and pilots on various topics. There was also a trip to Williams AFB, Arizona, to check out in an ejection seat on a special stand, and to experience a stint in a high altitude pressure chamber. The Williams trip was a mandatory portion of the training program; failure to withstand either the ejection seat or the high altitude chamber exercise resulted in automatic disqualification from school. Van had already passed ejection seat indoctrination at WADC in 1951, but welcomed the opportunity for more practice "banging out". In this business, one never knew when one might benefit from that experience.

Coming out of AFIT so recently, Van was advantaged in his academic work, as he had hoped. And his experience with the earlier test programs at Muroc were of use in his comprehension of flight test methods being taught. Midway through 52-A's performance phase, the students were treated to a lecture on rocket plane test procedures by NACA test pilot Joe Walker, who had flown the X-1 at supersonic speeds. It was not hard for Van to be enthused about what he was experiencing.

The way that TPS was structured early on, not all students finished on the same date; they graduated when, and only when, they passed all of the required courses, and completed all of the assigned test flights with passing marks on their associated reports. Eight of the nine students graduated 52-A on dates ranging from 22 August to 2 September, with one Air Force student having elected to enter combat in the Korean conflict. Van graduated on 29 August 1952.

At TPS, Van Shepard developed some lifelong friendships with his fellow students, not only from his own class but from other classes overlapping his. From 51-B was 1st Lieutenant Zeke Hopkins, a West Point graduate. From 51-C were Captain John Konrad, who would later become Chief Test Pilot at Chance Vought Aircraft, and

Captain Ray Popson, who would go on to fly the X-5 "swing-wing" research aircraft. From Van's own class 52-A was Major Al White, and from 52-B were Captain Fitz Fulton, a veteran of the 1948-49 Berlin airlift, and Captain Jimmy Joe Butler. Following graduation, all of these men except Butler and Shepard would continue on as test pilots with the Air Force Flight Test Center (AFFTC) at Edwards. Returning to the WADC in Ohio would be Van and Jimmy Joe, who would develop a close friendship.

These men knew that they were preparing themselves to put their lives on the line, in order to ensure that the United States would never fall behind in military air power. Some would go on after their military careers to do the same in the name of commercial aviation advancement. They all became members of a close-knit fraternity that would forever support each other, sometimes lean on another, and occasionally even bear pall for another.

TEN

Mach 1!

I T WAS RELATIVELY EASY for USAF Captain Van Shepard to reintegrate into the 2750th Air Base Wing at Wright-Patterson AFB in September 1952. He could continue doing all he had done eight months earlier, piloting testbed aircraft on which systems or components were being evaluated; but now, a fully certified test pilot, he could fly the actual experimental prototypes as well. He was, of course, already acquainted with the personnel, the facilities, the flight line, and the airspace around the Wright Air Development Center. At almost twenty-eight years of age, he finally considered this to be a "real job", which he figured would last more than a couple of years. Among his first orders of business were to buy a car and to rent a house on the south side of Dayton. The latter, likewise, he considered his first "real home" since childhood. Life was good.

Soon after his return, Van was able to attend ground school and check out in the North American F-86A Sabre. This formidable jet fighter had replaced the F-80 and F-84 as our primary warplane in the Korean conflict. His first experience in a swept-wing aircraft, Van could see and feel its superiority over more familiar aircraft from the moment he first advanced the throttle. He exceeded six hundred miles per hour, the fastest he had ever flown, on one of his familiarization flights.

Thereafter, Van found himself used as a test pilot for important validation programs underway at WADC. His next opportunity was in the Lockheed F-94C Starfire. The -C variant for a while had been coded F-97 as a separate program, as it represented such a significant upgrade from the -B model. In checking out, Van found himself familiar with the aircraft; to him it was like a "big brother" version of Lockheed's F-80. He was involved with the final tests certifying it for deployment as an "all-weather" fighter. He was one of the pilots to assess its engine flame-out flying performance, including the demonstration of unpowered or "dead-stick" landing capability.

After the Starfire program, it was back to the familiar Republic Thunderjet series, this time for the F-84G variant. Van would indeed remain involved with the "84" for quite a few years. In testing of the -G variant, he participated in a program to establish new aerial refueling capability for the Thunderjet. This was the first fighter to feature built-in capability for refueling using the relatively new flying boom system, in which a fuel delivery boom is "flown" down from the tanker to the receiving aircraft by an operator in the tanker's tail. This system was validated at WADC, and Van was the first pilot to demonstrate this type of refueling connection on a fighter aircraft. The F-84 team would later receive another reward of sorts: the -G variant was the first aircraft used by the new USAF "Thunderbirds" precision flight demonstration team.

For his Christmas 1952 furlough, Van headed back to Monroe. Among the first things he did upon his arrival was to visit his old elementary school, Sherrouse, to address the youngsters there about what it was like to fly an airplane. Unbeknownst to him at the time, a "relative-to-be" was in his audience: third-grader Marretta Heidenreich was the future sister-in-law of Frances Shepard! Thereafter, the family traveled to Arkansas to spend Christmas in Malvern with the Van Dusens; it was the first time Van had done so since 1945.

Back in Dayton, he achieved another milestone in his Air Force career, early in 1953. Officers who accumulate seven years as an active pilot, with at least two thousand flight hours, are awarded their "Senior Pilot's Wings", in which a star is added above the silver pilot's wings. Van received his in a ceremony at the WADC headquarters.

On Saturday, 16 May 1953, he was asked to participate in a demonstration during the annual Armed Forces Day Air Show at Wright-Patt. He enjoyed putting a Starfire through its paces for the assembled throng. It reminded him a bit of his days long ago showing off in the T-6 Texan; he loved acrobatics. He would be tapped regularly for demonstration flying throughout his tenure at Wright-Patt.

Meanwhile, halfway around the world, the Korean conflict was ending. After long negotiation, an armistice between the UN and the Communists was signed on 27 July 1953. The country would remain partitioned near the 38th parallel into the North and South Korean states. While US air patrols would continue in the area for many years, there would be no more combat.

Van received some bad news from Edwards in October. One of his buddies from Test Pilot School, Major Ray Popson, was killed on the 14th, in a crash of one of the two Bell X-5 research aircraft. The X-5 was the world's first aircraft able to alter the sweepback of its wings in flight. Popson was unable to recover from a spin which occurred when the plane's wings were in full 60° sweep. He left behind an expectant wife and a daughter. The incident had a profound effect on Van, reminding him of the mortality of the test pilot.

Life was changing fast for Van's siblings, Sam and Frances, in this time frame. Sam graduated from Louisiana Tech in 1953, with a business administration degree. He played varsity baseball, ran track, and was vice president of his graduating class. When a junior, Sam had met the love of his life, freshman Peggy June Walters, of Shreveport, Louisiana. After his graduation, the couple married on 18 July 1953 in Shreveport, with Van in attendance. Thereafter, Sam joined the Navy and graduated from Officer Candidate School in Newport, Rhode Island, followed by pilot school at Naval Air Station Pensacola, Florida. Peggy did not return to college; she liked to relate that she got her "MRS degree" in only two years. Sam would get his wings in late 1954; thus, all three Shepard boys were now involved in aerospace!

Frances married Navy Seaman Benny Heidenreich, the older brother of the aforementioned Marretta, on 30 January 1954, again with Van in attendance. She likewise graduated from Louisiana Tech, in 1954, with her degree in Home Economics.

Van received a once-in-a-lifetime opportunity in 1954. A North Korean pilot, Lieutenant No Kum-sok, had earlier defected with his brand-new MiG-15 jet fighter to a US base in Japan. The US took possession of the aircraft, and first tested it in Okinawa. It was then disassembled and moved to Wright-Patt, where it was examined in great detail by WADC engineers. Later, it was reassembled and restored to flying condition. Van Shepard was one of several pilots who then tested the aircraft, as part of extensive assessments of its performance against its primary competition, the North American F-86 Sabre. Each aircraft was found to have its strengths and weaknesses as combat fighters, with no clear winner. After completion of its assessments, the US offered to return the aircraft to North Korea, which did not respond. The plane was given to the Air Force Museum at Wright-Patt, and remains on display today in the museum's Korean War Gallery.

Also in 1954, building on successes achieved with the F-84 refueling program, Van became involved with a similar program for the Boeing B-47 Stratojet, America's first swept-wing bomber. The same flying boom fuel delivery process was being validated for the latest B-47 variant at McConnell AFB in Kansas. Van's role was to counsel the leadership and instructors on this refueling process from the pilot's perspective. He made several trips to McConnell, each lasting a few days.

On one of his first visits, Van went out to lunch with a USAF officer counterpart and his secretary, Diane Devins, a Boeing employee. Diane recalls that Van was in his flight suit, and that she immediately had eyes for him. Apparently the reverse was also true: they

Van & Diane making fudge, ca 1954

began dating during Van's visits. He would often drive her home from work, and eventually met her parents at their home in Fredonia, Kansas, about ninety miles away. But, alas, after the refueling program ended, the two would go their separate ways.

Van continued his flying at WADC throughout 1954, mainly on later variants of the F-84 and F-94 series. Each variant of an aircraft program had to be validated prior to its deployment into the US military, or its sale into foreign services. Production examples were subjected to many standardized tests of their flying performance, to prove their airworthiness. Van was one of several pilots at WADC performing these flying assessments.

The aircraft used in validation programs were periodically subjected to rigorous inspections, to ensure that they were safe for continued use in flight testing. Part of the inspection process was an evaluation flight, in which various specific maneuvers were made by the test pilot to ensure that the plane was behaving correctly. In one such assessment, Van was flying an F-84G, putting it through the routine series of maneuvers, when things went terribly wrong. The incident would be a watershed moment in his career, and is best described in his own words, from his report the next day:

> After taking off on a functional test flight for a periodic inspection in F-84G No. 52-3204, at approximately 1200E 6 April 1954, the right landing gear would not retract. The power was reduced and the gear cycled; on this attempt the gear retracted satisfactorily.
>
> A climb was started to altitude shortly after flying around at low altitude. At approximately 10,000 ft and 350 knots, a loud pressurization pulse was experienced with a high frequency vibration beginning immediately. The power was reduced to approximately 5,000 rpm and all engine instruments were read-

ing satisfactorily. My position was approximately 30 nautical miles NW of Wright-Patterson AFB. The tower was notified of the emergency and of the possibility of having to land at Richmond Airport, Indiana. The power was increased to 6,000 rpm, which seemed smoother than the 5,000 rpm setting. The vibration was light to moderate. Since the engine did smooth out somewhat at high power, the airplane was headed toward Patterson Field.

After approximately two or three minutes of flight, the tower asked me to turn on my parrot, Mode 2, and also wanted to know my altitude and whether I was IFR or VFR. I acknowledged VFR and approximately 6,000 or 7,000 ft. Shortly thereafter, at approximately 210 knots, a loss in power was noticed, with a decreasing of rpm and no power control response. It was evident then that I would not make Vandalia [James E. Cox Municipal] Airport, and I made a couple of slight turns to check terrain and possible emergency landing strips. Just as I was about to call the tower, smoke rushed into the cockpit from behind the seat; there was no fire warning. The battery was turned off. Then I looked over my left shoulder and observed smoke coming out of the top and left side of the fuselage at approximately the trailing edge station. My head was lowered in the cockpit and the canopy was jettisoned. Immediately there was a partial loss of lateral control as the plane went into a slight left bank (approximately 10-20°). The stick was not hard to move laterally as would be experienced from loss of aileron boost. At this time I looked back over my left shoulder and flames were now coming out with the smoke from the fuselage. I called "Mayday" several times on the radio, but there was no side tone, and as I was preparing myself for ejection, a complete loss of lateral and longitudinal control was experienced and the aircraft started into a steep left spiral. I ejected myself as the aircraft had rolled approximately 180°.

After my acceleration decreased, I was tumbling feet over

head rapidly, and it was a definite effort to bring my hands in to the body in order to pull the ripcord. The cord was pulled, but nothing happened. At this time I felt a binding at my abdomen and realized I was still fastened to the seat. The safety belt was released immediately, and almost simultaneously the chute opened, approximately 1,000 ft from the ground. Very shortly after that, I heard an explosion and looked downward to the right and behind me and there I saw an orange fire where the aircraft had hit the ground. I landed safely in a corner of a field (Garland Road and Route 721).

(signed)

7 April 1954   VAN H SHEPARD
Capt, USAF
24339A

Van was shaken but unhurt. He was assisted by a farmer and his wife, who were passing by and had seen his descent. They drove him to a general store where he called in to the base. He would relate that the flight control officer seemed surprised to hear his voice: the tower had not heard his "Mayday" call, and had assumed he had gone down with the aircraft.

This was to be the only incident which would qualify Van Shepard for the "Caterpillar Club", so named for the silk fabric in early parachutes which saved their users' lives. His accounts of his post-ejection struggles that day would help lead to automation of the seat separation process in fighter aircraft soon thereafter. He was cleared to resume flying.

Not long after the F-84 incident, Van became involved in testing of later variants of the F-86 Sabre. He had the fortuitous opportunity to fly the all-weather, higher-performance model, the "dash-D". This variant featured an uprated J47 afterburning turbojet, an aerodynamic radome nose, and other equipment changes. Van was happy to be reintroduced to the swept-wing hero of the Korean conflict. But there was more – oh, much more. During the course of his familiarization ride, he would check the box that every test pilot on earth hoped to check some day. He was allowed to ascend to altitude, begin a gradual descent, and "roll on the juice". The willing Sabre, its max'ed out afterburner screaming, just nudged past Mach One for those atmospheric conditions, at seven hundred miles per hour. Albeit in a shallow dive, Van Shepard had broken the sound barrier.

Back on the Wright Field flight line, his ground crew gathered to meet him as he climbed down from the cockpit; it was all hurrahs and backslaps. Later, he was presented with a certificate and lapel pin by North American Aviation, as a newly minted member of the "Mach Busters Club". He had accomplished supersonic flight in a production aircraft, less than seven years after it was done for the first time in a rocket-powered research plane! Such was the rapid progress being made in the world of aviation at the time.

ELEVEN

On to North American

RF-100A "Slick Chick" team, ca 1954

V AN WAS NOT ABLE to bask long in whatever glory there was for new supersonic test pilots. In the summer of 1954 he was dispatched to Suffolk County AFB, New York, for several weeks of testing on the newest Republic F-84 variant, the -F Thunderstreak. The only F-84 to feature swept wings, about half of the production of the "dash-F" was destined for NATO countries in Europe. Van was one of the pilots assigned to validate the aircraft for this service.

Suffolk County AFB was located on Long Island, and was responsible for air defense of the metropolitan New York City area.

While he was there, Van took the opportunity to do something special for his newly wedded sister Frances and her husband Benny. Following their January wedding, "Sis" had accompanied Benny to his station at the Newport, Rhode Island Naval Base, for the months that remained of his two years service. Following his discharge that summer, Van treated the couple to a few days in New York City. Each night, the three went out on the town, after which Sis and Benny returned to Louisiana.

Van's work with the Thunderstreaks in New York was not without some excitement. On the morning of 15 September, he was flying F-84F no. 52-6643 at 3,500 feet altitude over the Atlantic Ocean off Long Island. He was evaluating its performance with a special store (a releasable tank, weapon, or similar device) attached beneath its left wing. Normally, wing-mounted stores are attached and released in pairs, to maintain balance, but the aircraft must be proven safe to operate with only one. While maneuvering near the aircraft's maximum speed of 660 miles per hour, he suffered momentary loss of roll control, perhaps associated with the unbalanced effect of the single store. He was able to recover, but the high-G recovery maneuver caused the store to be ripped from beneath the aircraft and plunge into the ocean. He thus had his second air incident to report in five months, this one not as traumatic as the first.

He was glad to get back to Wright-Patt. In his absence, his base-ball team had competed in the WPAFB league tournament, and won it all! While he was disappointed to miss out on the opportunity to contribute, along with his teammates he was presented with a trophy.

Van joined a new validation program in the fall. Building on his work with the F-86 Sabre, he was assigned to begin testing the F-100 Super Sabre, also built by North American Aviation. As its name suggests, the Super Sabre drew from the F-86 Sabre design, but benefited from a much more powerful J57 engine. It was the world's first aircraft with supersonic speed capability in normal use.

Van checked out in the F-100A, and immediately began working with the RF-100A, a reconnaissance version of the aircraft. This program, also known as Project "Slick Chick", consisted of six production F-100A's modified with cameras mounted in faired compartments beneath the forward fuselage. Van did much of the test flying on the first aircraft so modified.

The USAF's experience with the Super Sabre was not without issues. The early variants suffered from an instability phenomenon called "inertia coupling", in which motion in one direction could cause unwanted motion in another, even resulting in loss of control or catastrophic structural failure in the extreme. The design had other problems as well. After several write-off incidents, at least one of them fatal, the Air Force grounded the -A models from November 1954 through February 1955.

The -C model intended to correct, or at least improve upon, many of these issues; its test and validation program at WADC was thus of critical importance. Van moved to the dash-C program, checked out (again exceeding Mach 1, this time in level flight), and spent several weeks flying its tests. Among them were engine flame-out tests, including emergency landing demonstration with no engine power: Van was the first pilot to perform a "dead-stick" landing on the -C model. He was also part of a team, which included his buddy Jimmy Joe Butler, that spent a few weeks in early 1955 at Eielson AFB in Alaska, validating its cold weather performance. The -C would be released to USAF squadron duty in the summer of 1955, albeit still exhibiting less than desirable flying characteristics. It would continue to be known as an unforgiving aircraft, until replaced by the much improved -D model a year later.

A new design trend in military aviation was gathering steam in 1955. The "delta wing" concept, which had been around for years, was noted in further research to be especially useful applied to supersonic aircraft. In addition to eliminating the separate horizontal stabilizer, its triangular shape inherently emulated a highly swept-back wing. Properly designed, this, in turn, afforded reduced aerodynamic drag, so important to supersonic aircraft.

The Wright Air Development Center was in the midst of this burgeoning trend. It was principally involved in the testing of the Convair YF-102A supersonic interceptor (the "Y" prefix indicating a second-level, more production-representative prototype than the "X"). In addition to its delta wing, this model was newly revised with a "Coke bottle" shaped fuselage, further enhancing its speed potential. Van Shepard was one of the WADC pilots selected to fly "The Deuce", as the plane was referred to by its team. He went through extensive ground school on the special characteristics of delta wing aircraft, and the F-102 in particular. One of the most significant differences flying a delta is the high angle of attack required for takeoff and landing, something its pilots must learn to execute. Van got his chance to fly one of the YF-102A prototypes on 3 May 1955. He exceeded the speed of sound in this aircraft as well, his third supersonic type. Little did he know that he would end up flying many hours in delta wing aircraft. The F-102 would later acquire the name Delta Dagger.

Van got an unusual treat on Saturday, 21 May 1955, Armed Forces Day. He was already looking forward to his usual participation in the Wright-Patterson Air Show, which always took place on that day. This year, he was asked to first fly his F-100 to the Port Columbus (Ohio) airport, to be a featured event in the North American Aviation (NAA) Columbus Division's Armed Forces Day celebration. This would be billed as a "homecoming" for the Super Sabre, produced at NAA's plant adjacent to Port Columbus. He then would return to Dayton and participate in the Wright-Patt show. Van eagerly accepted this "task".

At the appointed time, he took off from Patterson Field in F-100A #53-1576 and was over Port Columbus, 65 miles away, a mere nine minutes from wheels up. Carrying about 500 miles per hour, he dropped down close to the ground and advanced his throttle into afterburn. As he accelerated past, he glanced out of his canopy at the multitude gathered alongside. Onlookers would comment that they saw the jet fly past silently; then, invisibly trailing it by several hundred feet, they heard its earsplitting scream, its pitch dropping dramatically as it passed by due to extreme Doppler effect. He then pulled back and climbed nearly vertically.

Van came around, landed, and taxied up before sixty thousand admirers. He climbed out, traded his helmet for his officer's hat, and addressed the crowd with brief remarks about the virtues of the Super Sabre. He would then spend the next several minutes chatting with NAA Columbus engineers, frequently checking his watch. At the right time he took off for the return to  Wright-Patt. He then repeated the process for his home show, thus serving as an attraction in two different air shows over the space of about an hour! It was the first time the F-100 was featured as a flying participant in either show. The day was chronicled in local newspapers.

Meanwhile, Van's brother Sam had made great strides of his own in the US Navy. He had completed pilot school, and accepted a commission as a Lieutenant junior grade. Sam and Van got a kick out of the fact that they both had flown basically the same trainer aircraft: the Navy's SNJ and the Air Force's T-6 were almost identical. However, Van would forever be envious of Sam's aviation accomplishments in one sense: as a Navy pilot, Sam had made the obligatory six carrier landings, something an Air Force flyboy would never do.

After getting his wings, Sam entered and completed multi-engine school at Naval Air Station Hutchinson, Kansas. Thereafter, his graduating class was plowed back into multi-engine at Hutchinson as flight instructors; by early 1955 he was teaching basic, intermediate, and instrument flying to newly minted Navy pilots. Sam and wife Peggy had made Van an uncle yet again in March, with their first-born Greg (his fourth nephew – no nieces yet!).

NAS Hutchinson was only fifty miles from Wichita, where Van still had business with the refueling program at McConnell AFB. During his last trip in June 1955 to McConnell (and his last date with Diane Devins), Van made a point to visit Sam and family at Hutchinson. As he had not seen them since their wedding almost two years earlier, he had a great time just catching up, and meeting new nephew Greg.

In late summer 1955, Van's career would change direction. The 1950s was a time in which aviation was growing rapidly, like none other in its history. Remaining at the forefront of flying technology was of paramount importance to the military forces of each of the world's leading nations; this applied to fighters, bombers, and transport aircraft alike. And civil aviation was growing by leaps and bounds as well, especially in passenger transport. Every manufacturer had multiple military and civil aircraft development programs underway, and competition for orders from the military and the airlines was intense.

Competition for skilled test pilots to fly these development programs was also intense. Each such pilot had to have rare flying skills, instincts, and experience, and also be engineers of top caliber. Finding individuals with such a resume outside the military was unusual.

North American Aviation (NAA) was at the forefront of aviation design, with a long history of innovation and product performance in military bombers and fighters, both propeller-driven and jet-powered. On its drawing boards were many new, even more innovative designs. What it needed in the mid 1950s were pilots to test them.

NAA had earlier made its first bold move to this end. It hired Major Al White, Van's Test Pilot School 52-A classmate, away from the USAF to take over as chief test pilot at its Los Angeles Division in May 1954. White's principal assignment was to staff up the pilot ranks at the division. An early success was to hire Scott Crossfield, one of the nation's foremost test pilots, away from NACA in early 1955. Crossfield had been the first man to fly Mach 2, in the Navy's Douglas D-558-2 research aircraft in 1953; he was brought on specifically to fly NAA's upcoming X-15, the hypersonic research aircraft so advanced that it was really a spacecraft too.

Among the other pilots White went after was Van Shepard. Van pondered his offer to join NAA long and hard. He was happy as a USAF officer-pilot, getting the most exciting rides a pilot could hope for, including supersonic flights in three different types. But as a NAA pilot, his salary would be about twice as much as his Air Force pay, even including his flying bonuses. Further, he had held the rank of Captain for four years now, and was a bit frustrated with how long it typically took a test pilot to get promoted to Major. Despite his accomplishments, he had been told that this would not be imminent for him.

In addition, he would love to get back to California with its more flying-friendly climate. A year earlier, his brother Bill had resigned his government engineering position in Alabama and accepted employment with Chance Vought. He had moved his family to

Oxnard, California, to work on Vought's Regulus surface-to-air missile program for the Navy, at NAS Point Mugu. So Van, still the bachelor, would not be lacking family on the west coast should he make such a move.

He decided to accept NAA's offer as Engineering Test Pilot at the Los Angeles Division.

PART III

"Ride of the Valkyries"

Searchlight, Nevada, 7 March 1966, 9:19 am PST

The hearts of the two pilots sank. Thoughts of bailout again crossed their minds, but they quickly returned to their tasks at hand. They had to save this $750 million airplane (1960s dollars!). Following careful inspection of the landing gear, the chase pilots reported on the state of each, in their orchestrated downswinging and rotating deployment movements. They found that the nose gear had stalled a bit short of its full down travel, but was otherwise OK. The main gear were more problematic, to be expected given their much larger size and more complicated deployment kinematics. The right side four-tire wheelset did not complete its intended ninety degree rotation about its main strut. Thus the wheels were pointing a bit to the right of straight ahead. The left side was in worse shape -- the bogie beam, which carries the tire pairs in tandem, failed to pivot downward at all from its vertical orientation, leaving the rear tire pair positioned uselessly above the front tire pair, which in turn was positioned too low. They would have to try again.

Joe Cotton was instructed to attempt to raise the gear. Fortunately, utility system #1 hydraulic pressure was holding around 1,600 psi. He raised the lever to retract. The chase pilots reported that all gear indeed disappeared from view. Moments later, looking up from beneath the Valkyrie, Fitz Fulton reported that each gear appeared tucked away in its respective well. Edwards Data Control then directed Cotton to invoke the emergency extension system with the second try, which provided electric assist to the gear deployment hydraulics. This time, a bit of good news: a green light for the nose wheel! However, the earlier fate was again realized for each main gear, despite the additional electric assist.

Data Control called out, "OK, Zero-Zero-One, the engineers are hard after this. Please stand by."

With their crippled main gear hanging pathetically in partial deployment, Van Shepard and Joe Cotton crept on towards Edwards at 250 miles per hour, appearing to move even more slowly due to the plane's immense size.

The waiting became painful.

Several minutes later, Air Vehicle #1 was about a hundred miles east of Edwards. Shepard noted that the plane continued to fly normally. Nonetheless, the men had been in diligent, at times vehement, discussion as the engineers rendered their opinions on how best to handle the upcoming landing. There was urgency, with some impatience and anxiety, in the players' voices, but little manifestation of temper or anger. All involved knew that professional demeanor would give them the best chance to succeed.

The plan was for AV #1 to first jettison about 3,000 gallons (20,000 pounds) of fuel, lessening fire damage potential upon landing, and enabling the plane to land about seven percent lighter than scheduled. The team was already busy scrutinizing fuel levels in the seven tanks, and planning a jettison schedule that would maintain proper center of gravity during and after the release. This newly lightened configuration would, in turn, enable a reduced flare speed during landing. On cue, Cotton began to release fuel over the Mojave Desert 8,000 feet below.

The engineering team consensus was that Shepard's ninth left-seat landing of the XB-70 program would be his first on Rogers Lake, the large dry lakebed completely within the boundary of Edwards AFB. The lakebed is adjacent to the normal concrete runways, and as such has the full complement of emergency services available. The only concern was that it was still somewhat soft from above-average winter rainfall; however, a monitoring aircraft had made test landings a week earlier and pronounced it sufficiently firm. Landing on the lakebed, there would be no need for chutes or brakes after touchdown, which would have been partially functional at best, given both depended on the failed utility hydraulics. Shepard had already been assuming a lakebed landing would be his destiny. He had been replaying in his mind his right-seat landing on the lakebed in Air Vehicle #2 five months earlier, which went without incident. Under normal circumstances, it was actually easier to land on the lakebed than the runway, with so much wide open space available. Then again, these were hardly normal circumstances . . .

*　　　　*　　　　*

TWELVE

Betty

W ITH JUST A TOUCH of remorse, Van resigned his commission in the active duty US Air Force, effective 5 September 1955; he agreed to re-enter the Air Force Reserve, retaining his rank of Captain. He packed his belongings into a trailer behind his car, and started the long trip from Ohio to California. On the way, he spent a relaxing week with his family in Monroe. Business was booming at Shepard's, where Marie and a friend had opened a laundromat adjacent to the store. His sister Frances was teaching high school home economics, and her husband Benny, newly out of the Navy, had enrolled in Northeast Louisiana State College's physical therapy program.

Arriving in California in late September at almost thirty-one years of age, Van reported to his first real civilian job at North American Aviation's Los Angeles plant. Renowned for its World War II production of the P-51 Mustang, the plant was adjacent to the L.A. municipal airport, which would later become famous as "LAX". He rented a one-bedroom apartment nearby in a new building at 811 Cory Drive in Inglewood. He spent his first few days at L.A. Division getting oriented to corporate life and process. Van enjoyed making the acquaintance of fellow test pilot Scott Crossfield, of whom he was somewhat in awe: during his time with the High Speed Flight Station at NACA, Crossfield flew almost every research aircraft ever built in the United States. He would end up flying rocket-powered aircraft 87 times, the most of any pilot.

Van's first assignment would be in North American's ongoing F-100 fighter program. L.A. Division was busy building the first -D model prototype. This model was critical to the company, as it was to finally cure the design flaws that caused prior variants to be so challenging to fly. Van would be involved in flight testing of various -D model systems and subsystems installed in the older variant testbed planes, until the dash-D prototypes were ready to fly. These tests would be flown out of both the L.A. airport and the Air Force Flight Test Center (AFFTC) at Edwards. Van was happy to start out flying aircraft he was already familiar with.

He soon came to enjoy his new civilian life. It was made even easier by the fact that he was already acquainted with so many of his fellow pilots from Air Force days. He also loved his new proximity to family, after having been hundreds, if not thousands, of miles from his closest relatives for so many years. Not only was his brother Bill's family only about sixty miles away, but even closer was his cousin Lois Van Dusen Skarda and her family, in a northern suburb of L.A. There were many Sunday and holiday outings with family. And the money sure was nice; he was able to purchase a Ford Thunderbird after just a few months.

Van became involved with a new movement to establish a professional society for aviation engineer/test pilots. This group heretofore did not have an organization to advocate for their causes. This need was perceived in 1955 by a small group of individuals mostly in southern California, where many aircraft manufacturers were headquartered, and of course where many Air Force pilots were working as well. Van was invited to participate early in 1956, and attended some of the formative meetings. The group drew up articles of incorporation with the state of California as the Society of Experimental Test Pilots (SETP), which were approved on 12 April 1956. Van Shepard was inducted as a charter Associate Fellow, and would serve as the organization's secretary in 1958-59. The group would grow over its first sixty years to more than two thousand members in more than thirty countries. Van would remain involved in its leadership throughout his career.

Another dark day for those in the test pilot fraternity was 27 September 1956. AFFTC pilot Captain Mel Apt, another of Van's fellow AFIT and TPS graduates, was making his first flight in the Bell X-2 rocket-powered research aircraft at Edwards. After becoming the first person to fly three times the speed of sound, at Mach 3.2, he lost control of the plane during his unpowered homeward glide. He ejected in a special escape capsule, but was unable to get his parachute deployed. He was killed upon impact, leaving a wife and two young daughters. Van would attend another funeral for a buddy dying too soon in the service of his country.

Late that year, Van's expertise in aerial refueling was again put to use, this time on the F-100 program. He was assigned to fly tests to validate the concept of "buddy refueling" for the Super Sabre, using the -D model. In this method, the "thirsty" aircraft is refueled in midair by receiving a hose trailing from a "tanker" aircraft of the same type. In November 1956, Van was involved in the first such demonstration using two F-100s.

A bit of irony occurred in the fall of 1956. Chance Vought, brother Bill's company, was developing their latest and most capable surface-to-air missile, the Regulus II. This program was moved from NAS Point Mugu to the AFFTC at Edwards AFB, along with the group of electronics engineers, supervised by Bill Shepard, supporting it. So here was Bill, now working at Edwards, the most famous flight test venue of all, while his test pilot brother was based in Los Angeles!

While Van would often visit Edwards, both for engineering meetings and test flight activity, the brothers rarely saw each other at work. Nonetheless, Van would occasionally stop in on Bill's wife Lois in his travels between L.A. and Edwards: Bill, Lois, and sons Bill Jr., 6, Sam, 4, and Jeff, 3, had moved into a home in Lancaster, only twenty miles from Edwards. Lois recalls one occasion in which Van and Al White together stopped at the house for lunch.

During Christmas week 1956, the Mojave Desert was treated to a rare snowfall one evening. The next morning, Van came to visit Bill and family to exchange gifts. Afterwards, out in the front yard, he gave his nephews their first (and only) lesson on how to make a "snow woman"!

Living down the street from Bill and Lois was Murray O'Toole, an aeronautical engineer working for NAA, whom Van had gotten to know well. Also a bachelor, Murray was an avid skier, and convinced Van to give skiing a try that same winter. Somewhat reluctantly at first, Van accepted the challenge, and would become reasonably proficient, particularly for a Louisiana boy.

Back east, the extended Shepard family continued to grow. In 1957 Sam and Peggy were blessed with baby Julie, Van's first niece after four nephews. Sam discharged from the Navy in the fall and moved his family from Kansas back to Monroe, where he would enter the insurance business. Just as Van had, he maintained a commission in his branch's Reserve. Sister Frances and Benny likewise had a new baby girl, Fran, and moved to southern Louisiana where Benny began his physical therapy practice.

That year also saw Van's relationship with his best girlfriend, Betty Oberg, develop into something special. Betty was blond, tanned, and beautiful, seven years younger than Van, and reared in Los Angeles. She was the product of a proper Swedish family: her father, Lars, had immigrated from Sweden as young man, and her mother, Emmie, was born to a Swedish immigrant father in Washington state. Lars owned a construction company specializing in large civil engineering projects. He also owned a rental property in Inglewood, that happened to be across the street from Van's apartment; this is indeed how Van and Betty had met. The eldest of four children, Betty worked in the office of a medical practice in L.A. Also a skier, she and Van often made trips to the slopes when there was snow in the mountains. And best of all: Betty loved to fly.

New Years Day 1958 saw Van's family members in southern California gather at his cousin Lois's home in the San Fernando Valley. Present were Van and Betty, Lois Skarda and husband Joe with their teenage sons Larry and Joe Jr., and Bill and Lois Shepard with their three boys. Van and Betty took the occasion to announce their engagement to the family. They planned a June wedding.

Thereafter, his missile program winding down, Bill accepted a promotion to move to Vought's corporate headquarters in Dallas, Texas. He and Lois were happy to be able to live closer to their families in Louisiana. Though they would miss Van, they were pleased that he would soon have Betty looking after him. They left Lancaster for Texas in February 1958.

Van Huber Shepard and Betty Ann Oberg were married in Los Angeles on Saturday, 28 June 1958, attended by H. F. and Marie, Bill and Lois, Joe and Lois Skarda, and all of Betty's immediate family. It was a grand affair: the left side of the church looked like a beauty pageant; the right side looked like "Who's Who in Aviation". Betty's matron-of-honor was her sister Nancy Oberg Erwin; Van's best man was Al White, and one of his groomsmen Murray O'Toole. In the audience were several test pilots and aviation executives. Following their honeymoon, the couple rented a three bedroom home at 224 West Century Boulevard on the south side of Los Angeles, not far from the NAA plant.

THIRTEEN

Mach 2!

A3J Vigilante flight test team, 1959

V AN REMAINED ASSIGNED TO the F-100 program throughout 1958, and did most of his flying in support of many different kinds of testing on the various Super Sabre models. The last production variant, the dash-F, was a two-place trainer; Van flew many of its validation tests out of both L.A. and Edwards.

He also became involved with the Army's biological and chemical weapons testing at this time. The principal test site for this was the Dugway Proving Ground, in west-central Utah. The Army intended to equip F-100's as aerial spray vehicles, and ran many tests at Dugway assessing aerial dispersion characteristics, developing both the chemical agents and the aircraft nozzle designs. Van was dispatched to Dugway on 15 August 1958, and spent six weeks flying these tests. Almost all were conducted at night, when the atmosphere was calmest. The Army would then make measurements on the ground, assessing dispersal concentrations at varying distances from the spray zone.

Van took his bride with him for the six weeks. He was able to spend many daytime hours with Betty due to his night flying schedule. With so many empty square miles of rock-strewn terrain, he became interested in rock hounding. Betty was not quite so enthused, but often went along, as there was little else to do in the Utah desert. They had some success: they collected quite a few topaz stones, some with few flaws.

Back at L.A. Division, the big news in 1958 was the build of the first two of three X-15 research aircraft. The sleek little rocket plane, looking like nothing else in its satin black finish, was a point of great pride for NAA employees. Van was happy to be an "insider" to this program: his boss Al White had appointed himself backup to Scott Crossfield, the test pilot who would first fly it. Van was indeed privileged to be able to follow this program through his closest associates.

Rollout day was 15 October, when X-15 #1 was revealed to the public with pomp and circumstance. In the audience of invited guests and employees was Van Shepard. The principal speaker was Vice President Richard Nixon, who proclaimed that the X-15 had "recaptured the US lead in space", referring to its ability to fly higher than the altitude considered the threshold of space. This was an emotional time in the "space race", as a year earlier the Soviet Union had launched its Sputnik satellite, beating the US into orbit by three months. NAA would make headlines with the three X-15's for many years to come.

Early in 1959, another of North American's important new aircraft programs had reached the prototype stage. The A3J Vigilante was a two-place carrier-based attack bomber for the US Navy, with Mach 2 speed potential afforded by twin J79 afterburning turbojets. Its crew rode in a tandem arrangement, with the pilot in front and the bombardier-navigator behind, each with his own hatch and rocket-powered ejection seat. The aircraft featured a one-of-a-kind weapon system, in which up to three pieces of ordnance could be ejected in linear fashion out of the rear of the vehicle, between the two engines.

This was an advanced aircraft. It featured several "firsts" for production warplanes, including the first use of an on-board digital computer for navigation, and the first "head-up display", in which flight information is projected onto the windscreen in the pilot's field of view, so that he need not divert his focus downward.

The Vigilantes were being manufactured at NAA's Columbus, Ohio production facility. After successful completion of an experimental flight program using the first two air vehicles, Van Shepard was assigned as a program pilot for the pre-production test phase, for which the next nine builds were made available. As was typical, all manner of test flights were slated over 1959 and 1960. These flights were flown by a combination of Navy, NAA Columbus, and NAA Los Angeles pilots. Among the NAA pilots was another of Van's buddies from Test Pilot School, Zeke Hopkins, who had also joined NAA.

Unlike his Air Force test programs, which were almost always flown out of Los Angeles and Edwards AFB, this Navy program would have its test flights conducted over several venues across the country. In addition to L.A. and Edwards, some were flown out of Port Columbus, Ohio, and many out of the Naval Air Test Center at Patuxent River, Maryland. Other venues were used as well.

As he had not flown what was classified as a medium bomber

since the late 1940s, Van was eager, but also a bit apprehensive, about reintroducing himself to this class of aircraft. Nonetheless, in his first familiarization flight he exceeded Mach One, making the Vigilante the fourth type he had flown supersonically. With subsequent flights, he had the opportunity to explore higher and higher speeds and altitudes; it was not long before he had exceeded for the first time both 1,000 miles per hour and 50,000 feet.

In the spring of 1959, Van and Betty received sad news from Louisiana. Sister Frances had given birth prematurely to twin girls, Effie and Lillian, who lived but five hours. They were interred at the family grave site in Monroe alongside their aunt, Van's sister "Baby Jean".

Late in 1959, Van attained Mach 2, twice the speed of sound, for the first time in his career. This was about 1,350 miles per hour; it came during a flight out of Edwards in the fifth A3J-1 built, no. 146696. As was the case at Wright-Patt following his first Mach 1 flight, the occasion was cause for celebration back on the ramp at Edwards; he later would receive his Mach 2 pin from NAA.

Among Van's tasks as a Vigilante pilot was to establish a procedure for the "dead stick" landing. In a letter to his parents, he describes this experience, and the former Air Force pilot alludes to differences in working with the Navy now:

> My flying projects are developing techniques for "dead stick" landings, which is unusual for a twin-engine airplane as we never, never design for a double failure, but the NAVY says that fuel starvation or exhaustion is a single failure, so we have to demonstrate. We are now practicing and building up by determining flare speeds with both engines in "idle". Of course we start at the high speeds, 200 KIAS [Knots Indicated Air Speed]

first. We have successfully demonstrated down to 160 KIAS at 41,000 lbs but I believe the specification calls for 151 KIAS at 42,000 lbs. The final landings will be done at Rogers Dry Lake, Edwards AFB.

Letter from California, 4 March 1960

Apart from the dead stick landings, Van's principal assignment in the pre-production Vigilante was to seek out and identify any inertia coupling tendencies. Ever since the phenomenon so troubled the early F-100 variants, all new aircraft designs were scrutinized for it early in their development cycles. All plausible speed and altitude combinations had to be evaluated by test pilots; thus many flights were required. Van's daily flight plan called for several maneuvers that would only be executed in emergency situations, but had to nonetheless be explored to ensure the Vigi's airworthiness. Later in the same letter, he describes this test program:

My main project right now is inertia coupling investigation, or what we call "roll coupling". This is a real slow, long program, as every two weeks or so we have to stop and let the Computer Section catch [up] with Flight Test. This investigation is accomplished by doing fast rolls, full deflection, at ever increasing critical Mach numbers and altitudes. Coupling means just what it says, that is, [as] an airplane, especially high density, rolls real fast 150-200 deg/sec, it begins to yaw or pitch, slowly at first, but divergently, and this excursion will couple into the other axis abruptly, and then the airplane is out of control.

Letter from California, 4 March 1960

Van had long hoped to own his own airplane someday. Betty, also a flying buff, supported the notion from early on, so it was merely a matter of establishing sufficient budget to make the purchase. But

Van had always practiced diligent stewardship of his financial resources, ever since that attempt at saving for his first airplane ride. It took a while for him and Betty to be ready to take on this type of discretionary expense.

Van had his eye on the four-place Cessna 172 ever since it was introduced in 1956. In the winter of 1959-60, the used airplane market was beginning to see a few 172's for sale. Studying the listings, he found one that looked promising. On his test ride he took Betty, who endorsed its purchase, and Van became an aircraft owner at long last.

For the first several months, the couple lived like vagabonds, leveraging their new mode of transport. There were many trips to the Sierra Nevada, for skiing in the winter and camping in the summer. There were trips as far away as Mexico, and even a visit to the 1960 Winter Olympic games at Squaw Valley, California. One or more of Betty's siblings would often tag along on the more local trips. Van also used the Cessna for a "stag" ski weekend to Mammoth Mountain with Murray O'Toole and Al White; there was nothing quite like an airplane trip with a designated driver available! However, soon enough, Van and Betty realized that their wanderings were beginning to tax their budget. They were hoping to move into a more upscale neighborhood as soon as practical, and were now saving toward this. Accordingly, they decided to curtail their wanderlust a bit.

Van continued to spend most of his test hours with the A3J program. By March 1960 he had totaled eighty hours in the Vigilantes. Al White, in order to utilize his test pilots to the fullest, sent some for hi-G training at the Naval Air Development Center in Johnsville, Pennsylvania. This facility operated the largest human centrifuge in the world at the time, which could generate accelerations up to the limit of human tolerance, and beyond. Van Shepard was one of the pilots spending a week in the centrifuge program in the spring of 1960.

Soon after returning from Johnsville, Van was discharged from the Air Force Reserve, on 31 May 1960. His Air Force service, including both active duty and reserve, totaled exactly seventeen years. At the age of thirty-five, he was now a full-fledged civilian, for the first time in his adult life.

Later in 1960, back at North American Aviation, the Vigilante program was taking a new turn. The Navy decided to abandon its plan for the Vigi as an attack bomber, in favor of a reconnaissance role. Several design changes were to be made for the new configuration, which would have to be re-validated. But rather than extend Van Shepard's role in its testing, NAA decided to move him into a new program, the Sabreliner.

The Sabreliner was a small, swept-wing, twin turbojet passenger aircraft. It was designed to be configurable into multiple variants, including civil models, thus enhancing its profitability potential to NAA. It was capable of speed competitive with that of commercial jets. Already in production were jet trainer/transports for the Air Force and Navy (T-39 and T3J respectively). The planned civil variants were to be executive transports for both government and corporate fleets, and a luxury private jet. The latter was intended to compete with several new executive jet designs in the works, including one by inventor Bill Lear.

Van Shepard was named lead program pilot for the flight testing of the civil models, which included a significant additional role: he was to have signatory responsibility for Federal Aviation Agency (FAA) type certification required for the civil variants, meaning he would be the person who would authenticate all flight test documentation used for compliance with FAA requirements.

He was pleased to have earned the additional responsibility with this new assignment. However, it represented quite a departure from his history with NAA. He had never in his career tested anything other than military aircraft. His role with the Sabreliner would open up many new considerations in his day-to-day activity: he would have to interface with civilian customers, with those associated with commercial flying infrastructure, such as airports and fuel suppliers, and of course with the FAA. In his certification responsibility, he would have to deal with paperwork to a greater extent than he ever had, not something he looked forward to.

But as he began to familiarize himself with the aircraft, in production T-39 models, he noted that there were going to be advantages to this assignment: the Sabreliner had far more creature comfort built-in than anything he had ever flown. Even the no-frills military variant was smooth, quiet, and spacious compared to the combat aircraft he was accustomed to. And these attributes would only get better in the civil variants. He decided that he could get used to this kind of flying!

For a transport aircraft, the Sabreliner was quite the performer. It was capable of 550 miles per hour, and could land on short runways, by virtue of its combination of small size and use of thrust reversers built into its jet engines. Van would spend most of the next two years on the civil Sabreliner "cert" program.

In the meantime, he and Betty were going through a period of extreme emotions.

On the high side, they had found that home they were seeking. They bought a ranch-style house in the area known as Mandeville Canyon, in the foothills of the Santa Monica Mountains, in west L.A. They were fortunate to be able to find an affordable place there, at 2186 Mandeville Canyon Road: with only two bedrooms, the home had limited marketability, but was perfect for the two of them. It was ideally located, a manageable drive south to the NAA plant, but also in the direction of Edwards AFB, where Van spent considerable time. The beach at Santa Monica, a special attraction for Betty, was only fifteen minutes away, and Van Nuys Municipal Airport, where Van kept the Cessna, only thirty.

But the couple also experienced personal tragedy in this same time frame. Following the conception of their first child, Betty suffered greatly from what was diagnosed as a tubal pregnancy, which had to be terminated. She and Van never conceived again.

FOURTEEN

Valkyrie

With the Sabreliner, ca 1963

THROUGH THE LATE 1950s and into 1960, the X-15 program was not the only high profile aircraft program underway at North American Aviation. In December of 1957, NAA had won a long, hard-fought competition with other manufacturers to design and build a heavy bomber for the US Air Force that could fly at three times the speed of sound. This aircraft was intended to eventually replace the B-52 as the USAF's main intercontinental nuclear weapon delivery vehicle. NAA's winning submission featured a long-necked fuselage, the largest delta wing ever designed before or since, a canard foreplane for managing pitch trim, and an innovative technology called compression lift, which intended to improve lift-to-drag ratio at high supersonic speeds. It was to be powered by six newly designed General Electric J93 turbojets capable of continuous afterburn, arranged side-by-side in the aft of the fuselage. Inevitably, the engines would be referred to as the "six pack". One of the most exotic aircraft ever designed, it would be designated the B-70.

A name was selected for the aircraft in 1958, via an Air Force-wide contest. The winner: "Valkyrie", a mythological Norse war goddess who roamed the skies above battling tribes below, deciding which of the victims would go to "Valhalla", the warrior's heaven.

The Los Angeles Division, which had B-70 design and development responsibility, was hard at work in 1960 designing the aircraft and planning its pre-production build and testing programs. The problem was, this was going to be the costliest warplane program in US history, by far. It was reviewed many times in Washington by all stakeholders, including the various USAF commands, the Joint Chiefs of Staff, the Secretary of Defense, the Congress, and the President himself. Elements of the program would be reconfigured, canceled, and reinstated multiple times. As one of the last actions of the Eisenhower administration at the end of the year, a decision was made that the production program would be sustained. There would be twelve prototypes fabricated for development testing, with first flight occurring in 1962.

In response, in early 1961, Al White was designated as B-70 chief program pilot. He was coming off his backup role to Scott Crossfield as pilot for the X-15 contractor tests, never having to substitute for Crossfield. Former Navy pilot Al Blackburn was named backup to

White in the B-70. Due to the number of vehicles in the prototype program at the time, NAA decided that they needed additional test pilots, in order to cover what was expected to be a busy test program.

As Van Shepard watched these events unfold, he wondered if he might indeed be tapped for the program. After all, he had recently come off another high performance bomber program, the A3J Vigilante. Though he was still busy with Sabreliner certification, he could not see NAA being able to cover the B-70 without using him or hiring more pilots. Al White wanted him on the program. Sure enough, it was not long before Van was assigned as an engineering test pilot. Added at the same time was Zeke Hopkins.

To say that these pilots were excited about their involvement in this edge-of-the-envelope program is an understatement. To a man, they perceived it to be the ultimate opportunity in their flying careers. They immersed themselves with enthusiasm into the myriad familiarization activities. There were design meetings, aerodynamics lectures, subsystem meetings at suppliers, meetings with the USAF. There were also simulators up and running: the pilots began to gain experience in a flight controls simulator, and an "Iron Cross" rig, which simulated aircraft motions for a pilot in an actual cockpit mockup. The pace was rapid, as the first prototype flight was as close as eighteen months away.

This level of activity did not last long. A new administration had taken over in Washington, DC. Early in the Kennedy executive office, it became clear that the B-70 program was under close scrutiny. Indeed, word came down in April 1961 that the B-70 would not proceed to serial production. Notwithstanding, President John Kennedy was keen on the wisdom of exploring Mach 3 flight in large aircraft. Apart from its importance to defense preparedness, he also believed that supersonic passenger travel was coming, and strongly desired that American aircraft industry be in competitive readiness.

His administration thus directed that NAA continue with the build and testing of three B-70 prototype vehicles, the first to fly in 1964.

Responding to this cutback, changes were made in the pilot assignments. The prototype program would continue on, with Al White as chief program pilot. But due to a conflict of interest situation, Al Blackburn had to resign NAA, and was replaced with Zeke Hopkins as White's backup. Van Shepard was released back to his Sabreliner certification job, after only a few months of B-70 program familiarization work. The pilots had always recognized that the B-70 was on less than solid footing due to its great cost; the scope reduction came as no surprise.

It was during this period that the United States finally sent a man into space. On 5 May 1961, Navy Commander Alan Shepard made his fifteen minute suborbital flight aboard the Mercury capsule "Freedom 7" atop a Redstone booster. Van Shepard would become somewhat weary of explaining to others that he was not related to America's first man in space. But it was notable that among the original "Mercury Seven" astronauts, the two USAF pilots, Virgil "Gus" Grissom and Gordon Cooper, were graduates of both AFIT and the USAF Test Pilot School, just as Van was. He would wonder if he could have been a candidate for the Mercury program, had he remained in the Air Force. Ah, but that asthma history could well have surfaced in the rigorous astronaut medical qualification process.

Now off the B-70 program, Van tried to use the newly less frenetic pace of his work life to improve his relationship with Betty, and to renew his connection with family. In the summer of 1961, the couple made their longest cross country trip to date in the Cessna. They took a week-long vacation, visiting Texas, Louisiana, and Arkansas, introducing Betty to many members of Van's family who were not able to attend their wedding. In each location, Van ended up giving rides in the Cessna to all that wanted one. And while in Louisiana, they met three new nieces and nephews for the first time: Sam's Wendy and Mark, and Frances's Sonja.

Later, at home in California, Van and Betty were beginning to really enjoy life in their new Mandeville Canyon setting. This was an exclusive area; it was home to many in the entertainment business and others of high social standing, several of whom were avid private pilots and aircraft owners. Word had gotten around that one of the new residents was a test pilot for North American. It was not long before Van and Betty became close personal friends with two neighbor couples who shared their passion for aviation. One was actor/director Dick Powell and his wife, actress June Allyson, who lived on a 48 acre ranch called Amber Hills. The other was Dave Maytag, grandson of the founder of the Maytag washing machine enterprise, and his wife Jean. These couples would take flying vacations together in each other's aircraft, including fishing expeditions to Mexico, where Betty once caught a marlin in the Pacific.

In May of 1962, an organizational change at Los Angeles Division would yet again affect Van's career path. Zeke Hopkins, the backup pilot for the XB-70 (as it was now referred to), was promoted to a new position as chief of NAA test operations at Edwards AFB. His replacement as XB-70 backup pilot was Van Shepard. So, after about a year away from the program, it was right back into it for Van.

Also newly assigned to the program were the Air Force project test pilots: in the lead was Lieutenant Colonel Joe Cotton, and his backup was another buddy of Van's from Test Pilot School, Major Fitz Fulton. Both men were career test pilots. Cotton had been lead USAF pilot on the Convair B-58 Hustler flight test program. The trainer variant of the Hustler, the TB-58A, was to serve as the primary chase plane for the XB-70. Fulton had long been flying with the Bomber Operations Branch of the Flight Test Directorate at Edwards, and also had many hours in the B-58.

Van worked hard to catch up in the XB-70 program. He had much to do, as things had moved rapidly in his absence. There was a full scale mockup in place at Los Angeles. The assembly of the first prototype, Air Vehicle #1, was underway; the build site was the USAF's Plant 42 manufacturing facility in Palmdale, California, about sixty miles north of L.A. Major sections of the fuselage had been delivered, and were about to be mated together.

Among the first orders of business for Van in his new position was to learn to fly the Hustler, as he would usually be flying chase whenever he wasn't in the Valkyrie. Al White did not have B-58 experience either, so both pilots would attend the B-58 school at Carswell AFB, Texas, in June 1962.

Van decided to spend the weekend prior to the start of school with his brother Bill and family, at their new home in Arlington, Texas, flying in from L.A. on Friday, 1 June. He had a great time with his nephews as always, and also got to meet his newest niece, six-month-old Amy. He then joined his boss, who flew in on Sunday, at their hotel in nearby Fort Worth. The two then attended the B-58 Senior Officer Course at Carswell for the following three weeks.

The Hustler, first deployed to squadron service in 1960, was the world's fastest intercontinental bomber at the time, the only one capable of Mach 2. It was classified as a medium bomber, featuring a delta wing design and four General Electric J79 turbojets mounted on underwing pylons. It also had a unique jettisonable underbelly pod, which housed additional fuel and, when armed, the warhead. The aircraft normally carried a crew of three, seated in tandem. There was also a trainer variant called the TB-58A, in which the instructor position was located close behind the student-pilot in a mid cabin with greater window area.

The Hustler would serve dual purposes for the XB-70 program. First, as the largest delta wing aircraft in US service, it would allow the Valkyrie pilots to gain needed experience flying such vehicles, with their greater angles of attack required for takeoff and landing. Second, with its greater speed and range capability, it would serve as an effective chase plane for the XB-70. Shepard and White thus particularly benefited from the use of the TB-58A trainer during their time at Carswell.

The two pilots had hoped to log another Mach 2 ride out of their experience, but it was not to be. Carswell was not interested in dealing with the extra wear-and-tear that multiple maximum-speed runs would impart to the engines in their trainer fleet. While all of the students would go home somewhat disappointed in this regard, the Hustler nonetheless became the fifth supersonic type flown by Van, and the largest aircraft he had flown to date.

His last week of the three was an eventful one on the personal side as well. His other brother Sam and wife Peggy had come to Texas for a visit with Bill and Lois and with Van, who was able to slip out one weekday evening and join the family for dinner in Fort Worth. And then, as B-58 school was ending on Friday, 22 June, Betty flew to Forth Worth along with White's wife. The two couples spent an enjoyable weekend together, highlighted by a dinner party on Sunday put on by Bill and Lois at their home. The four returned to California on Monday the 25th.

Author's Note:

My uncle's 1962 trip to Texas for B-58 school provided me with my most enduring memories of him, sustained by the fact that I kept a daily diary at the time, which I still have. I was twelve years old, fresh out of sixth grade, and vividly remember that first weekend he spent with us: waiting for him in the front yard on Friday evening, and him pulling up in a white car.

Although there were probably others, that was the only time I can recall sleeping under the same roof as Van. I gave up my bedroom for him, and slept with my brothers, Sam and Jeff, in their room. We four guys had the whole upstairs to ourselves; the evening scene was something like a sleepover. The next morning he educated us on the benefits of brushing with tooth powder – I recall him teaching us the jingle "Start the day with Py-Co-Pay".

My brothers and I were quite into baseball at the time, as was Van. I played Little League, and would often play pitch & catch with my brothers in the back yard. We had had our eyes on an expensive catcher's mitt at the local sporting goods store for a long while. On Saturday, Van took us to the store and bought us that mitt.

When he returned with Betty on the 24th for the dinner party, Van took us straight to that same store and bought us a catcher's mask, to go along with the mitt.

We were sad when he had to go back to California.

FIFTEEN

Maiden Flight

Fulton, Shepard, Cotton, & White at the XB-70 rollout, 1964

W HITE AND SHEPARD RETURNED to find good progress on the build of XB-70 Air Vehicle ("AV") #1. It was starting to look like a real airplane, albeit wingless for the moment. That fall the landing gear were installed, and the vehicle was moved outdoors on its own wheels to be repositioned for final assembly.

The pilots would frequently visit Palmdale to watch the build, and to provide input to manufacturing decisions where flight character could be affected. But most of their time was spent in Los Angeles in design meetings and on the simulators. They also traveled to supplier facilities and to USAF test facilities where various systems were undergoing development and validation.

They were also involved with the new J93 jet engine under development for the Valkyrie. At the time, this was one of the most powerful turbojet engines ever developed. The supplier, General Electric, had early engines under test in 1962 at its Evendale, Ohio facility, as did the Air Force at its Arnold Engineering Development Center at Arnold AFB, Tennessee. All four of the program pilots, White, Shepard, Cotton, and Fulton, would often travel to these facilities for meetings, to witness significant tests, and to participate in experiments in which actual pilot input was involved.

Later on, while the build continued on AV #1, first deliveries of subassemblies for the second prototype were received at Palmdale. Soon enough, the build of AV #2 would begin with fuselage section mating operations. On 22 October 1962, the Air Force re-designated the prototype aircraft as XB-70A, the suffix "A" being added to reflect the changes from the design originally approved.

On the personal side, Van and Betty got to see Bill as he visited Los Angeles in January 1963. He was there to interview for a leadership position in the defense industry. He was extended an offer, which he later declined. During their visit, the brothers toasted the arrival of their newest niece, Frances's Heidi.

Also in January, Van and Betty were saddened by the death of their Mandeville Canyon neighbor and flying companion Dick Powell, who succumbed to lung cancer at the age of 58.

While Van was becoming busier with the Valkyrie assignment, he continued to ride herd on the Sabreliner certification program. He was quite relieved when, in April 1963, NAA received its type certificate from the Federal Aviation Agency, declaring the civil Sabreliner ready for commerce. Van's work completed, sales of the aircraft would commence immediately. While he could now focus all of his energies on the XB-70A, he would later be gratified to note that among the Sabreliner's customers was no less than the White House. One T-39A would carry the call sign Air Force One: late in his presidency, Lyndon Johnson would regularly use no. 62-4478 to get into and out of his Texas ranch. Today, this aircraft is on display at the National Museum of the USAF.

It was in this period in their marriage that Van and Betty began to have serious difficulty. While Betty knew what she was getting into marrying a test pilot, the time demands of Van's job were increasing in locked step with his responsibility. There would be nights when Van worked so long into the evening that he never returned home. The pace of new aircraft programs was such that development and testing work was, at times, practically a 24-hour endeavor, and pilot input was always at a premium. This was especially problematic for those working at Palmdale or Edwards while trying to live in L.A. (Edwards even had a barricks-like overnight facility just for such situations). Without children around, and weary of being alone, Betty naturally developed a reliance on endeavors outside the home, be they employment, volunteer activities, recreational activities, travel, or relationships.

The couple remained together, but, sadly, developed separate sets of friends and interests over time, and began to take separate vacations. Betty was fond of tropical beaches, and would find it difficult to turn down invitations to join friends in remote destinations. Van, in turn, continued to expand upon that affinity for Hispanic cultures that was kindled during B-26 school near Del Rio. Later in 1963, he took a vacation to Central America. He had been cultivating an interest in Latin American anthropology, and used the trip to bolster his collection of pre-Columbian artifacts. He purchased numerous pieces, including clay figurines and pottery, and polished stone arrowheads, all documented as authentic. The clay pieces were donated by Van's mother Marie to the University of Louisiana at Monroe in 1984, and are on display at the Museum of Natural History there. During the same trip, Van somehow made the acquaintance of none other than Bing Crosby.

There was to be yet another cutback applied to the XB-70A program. The build of the third prototype, AV #3, was canceled on 5 March 1964. Even though much of the material for the vehicle had been delivered or was being fabricated by suppliers, significant savings were realized by cancellation of the assembly of the aircraft.

This change did not affect test pilot staffing for the flight program; it was felt that two company pilots and two Air Force pilots would still be required to sustain an experimental program based on two proto-types instead of three.

Monday, 11 May 1964 was a magical day for North American Aviation and those working on the Valkyrie program, including Van Shepard. It was the day that Air Vehicle #1 was rolled out of its assembly hanger to meet the world for the first time. In front of a large invited audience at Air Force Plant 42 in Palmdale, the completed AV #1 was towed out into the sunshine, cameras clicking away. Just sitting there, serial number 62-0001 almost looked like it was flying at Mach 3. USAF and NAA officials, including the four pilots, were gathered at a podium, at which speeches were made describing AV #1 and her forthcoming mission. Afterward, the audi-ence was permitted to walk beneath the giant white aircraft for a closer look. The pilots freely circulated and answered questions; Van made a point of connecting with several children, to whom he happily described his new mount.

The next day, the development work began. AV #1 had to have all of its systems checked and rechecked indoors, then move on to weeks of engine starts and runups at an outdoor hard stand. Next, on Plant 42's airport taxiways and runways, there were taxi tests, simu-lated takeoff runups, and simulated landing rollouts, before the Valkyrie would be ready for her maiden flight. Along the way, there were many changes to be implemented to both hardware and control strategies for this most complex aircraft ever assembled.

The pace of the development work was strenuous, and hard on the engineers, technicians, pilots, and their families. That summer, there were nights in which Van literally slept in the cockpit of AV #1, as the engineers and technicians working below would need a pilot to flip a switch or move a lever every so often; it didn't make sense to make the seventeen foot descent of the stairs, only to have to climb back up again moments later.

A welcome respite from the development work for Van was the proficiency flying he was able to do in the Air Force Flight Test Center's TB-58A Hustler at Edwards. This aircraft, #55-0662, would be the chase plane for the XB-70A flight program. During Van's proficiency flights, it indeed became the second Mach 2 type appearing in his log book.

Later that summer, on 1 September 1964, Van was honored with his induction as a Fellow grade member in the Society of Experimental Test Pilots.

Finally, AV #1 was ready for her maiden flight, on Monday, 21 September 1964. The four pilots worked all day Sunday the 20th at Palmdale, getting ready. The pilot for the flight would be Van's boss Al White, with recently promoted Colonel Joe Cotton as copilot. Lieutenant Colonel Fitz Fulton (also recently promoted) would pilot the TB-58A chase, with Van Shepard as his copilot. White and Shepard rented motel rooms nearby on Sunday evening, so they could be at the plant at 4:30 am Monday.

After the four met briefly at Palmdale, Fulton and Shepard drove to Edwards to prepare their TB-58A for flight. There would be a near-squadron of supporting aircraft heading from Edwards to Palmdale for the maiden flight. In addition to the TB-58A, there were four T-38 Talon jets flying chase (one serving as a photo plane), a C-130 Hercules, and a medical helicopter. The crews boarded their respective aircraft at 6:00 am, and monitored AV #1's startup progress on the radio from Palmdale. At one point, the Valkyrie had started its engines and looked like a "go"; Fulton began taxiing out the Hustler (the flight from Edwards to Palmdale was less than five minutes). However, it proved a false alarm, and the Hustler returned to the ramp. Finally, the call came just after 8:00 am that AV #1 was taxiing, and all of the support aircraft left for Palmdale.

Arriving over Plant 42, Fulton was cleared to circle the airport, and he and Shepard watched with anticipation as the giant delta lined up at the foot of Runway 07 below. Coordinating with White and Cotton via an open radio channel, Fulton had the Hustler positioned alongside the Valkyrie as it rotated and took to the skies at 8:25 am. Though it lifted off at over 200 miles per hour, due to its great size it looked like it was barely moving, an illusion that those associated with the program would get accustomed to. At 189 feet long, the XB-70A was the second longest aircraft ever to fly at the time, and *the* longest to fly over seventy feet high: Howard Hughes's 219-foot H-4 flying boat, the "Spruce Goose", only reached an altitude of about seventy feet on its one and only flight in 1947.

For its maiden flight to Edwards, where it would reside for its development program, the team had hoped to achieve supersonic speed, in order to collect a bonus from the Air Force for doing so. But it was not to be: there were multiple problems during the flight, not the least of which was landing gear that would not retract, preventing any notion of exceeding Mach One. Then upon landing, a brake locked up, which caused a small fire during rollout. But problems such as these are not uncommon on maiden flights, and it was pronounced successful.

The Valkyrie would exceed Mach One on its third flight, three weeks later. The first five flights of the XB-70A program would all be piloted by White and copiloted by Cotton. For each of the five, Shepard and Fulton would swap pilot and copilot duties in the TB-58A chase plane. At the end of its fourth flight, AV #1 landed back at Palmdale, for four months of structural testing and a new paint job at Plant 42.

SIXTEEN

Double Shifts

A V #1 TOOK TO THE air again on 16 February 1965, returning to Edwards from Palmdale. Beginning with the next flights, Fitz Fulton and Van Shepard would get their first rides in the Valkyrie. Fulton sat in for Joe Cotton as copilot on 25 February, with the latter joining Van in the chasing Hustler. Since a problem cut short this flight, Fulton was granted another ride on the next.

Van got his turn at copilot on the eighth flight, on Wednesday, 24

March. He was pleased to have the honor of rolling on the power for takeoff. Having six throttles with a total of 180,000 pounds of thrust at your fingertips was an experience not to be forgotten; the XB-70A was, at the time, the most powerful aircraft ever flown. However, due to its weight, its acceleration did not feel all that brisk; indeed, this flight was the first in the program (and in the history of aviation) in which the aircraft weighed more than 500,000 pounds at takeoff.

That day White and Shepard would exceed Mach 2 for the first time in the program, at 1,365 miles per hour. The copilot's main endeavors during the flights were to monitor temperatures and pressures in the various systems, control the air intakes for the engines, and schedule fuel delivery from the seven tanks in order to maintain proper center of gravity. In addition to merely flying the plane, the pilot was busy following a preset speed, climb, and path schedule, and performing various control inputs to which the response of the aircraft was recorded. Their tasks were continuous and demanding; neither man would have even one minute to take in the view. But this flight of the Valkyrie, Van's third Mach 2 type, was the most exciting he had ever made in his life to date.

Al White would continue to pilot all of the first sixteen flights of the program, with Cotton, Fulton, and Shepard rotating as copilot. With the size and fuel capacity of the Valkyrie, many aviation records for takeoff weight and time at speed would be broken and re-broken, as they pushed the performance envelope out toward their aircraft's design goals. As the chasing Hustler was only capable of Mach 2, it would often be left behind by the XB-70A. Typically, it would peel inside of the Valkyrie's flight path, short-cutting its oval-shaped course, and rendezvous later in the flight as the faster aircraft decelerated.

On Van's second flight, the eleventh of the program on 28 April 1965, there was some excitement after landing. The crew performed a scheduled "hot soak" test of the tires, in which the aircraft stands for several minutes just off the end of the runway after rollout. The drag chutes were not used in the landing, in order to evaluate worst-case brakes heating into the tires. Tremendous heat is generated in decelerating the 150 ton aircraft from 200 miles per hour to zero without chutes. One by one, three of the eight maingear tires blew during the soak. As a result, the aircraft could not be taxied to its hanger, and was too far away for an egress stairway to be brought up. Each pilot had to exit the airplane via a device called the "Sky Genie", which lowers him the seventeen feet to the ground via a controlled rope descent.

On Sunday, 23 May 1965, Edwards AFB hosted an Armed Forces Day open house for family members. Prominently featured on the flight line was a static display of AV #1. Van was finally able to have Betty see his bird up close and personal at this event. While she was impressed with the imposing stance of the giant aircraft, Van could sense a certain disdain for this machine that had taken away so much of her husband's life. It was quite understandable.

Meanwhile, the build team was completing the assembly of Air Vehicle #2 in Palmdale. The two prototypes were almost identical, the main exceptions being a slightly different wing configuration, more fuel capacity, and automated inlet duct control in AV #2. The most significant difference, however, was that #2 was simply put together better, having had all the learnings from the build and test of #1 applied. The new bird, carrying serial number 62-0207, was rolled out on 29 May 1965 with less fanfare than #1, but the event was again attended and enjoyed by the four pilots.

Ground development of #2 began the next day, just as it had for #1. The pilots would now struggle more than ever with their schedules, having to cover both the flights of #1 at Edwards and the ground testing of #2 at Palmdale. Van was copilot to White for #1's fourteenth flight on 1 July, which was memorable: they achieved Mach 2.85, the program's fastest yet, and set an aviation record for the longest continuous supersonic time at one hour, nineteen minutes. The downside of the day was that Van had to then drive to Palmdale and work the afternoon shift supporting #2's ground tests.

Early in July, Van was excused from the XB-70A flight program for a few weeks, to indoctrinate on a new assignment at NAA. Los Angeles Division was building a special air vehicle, the Vertical Take Off and Landing (VTOL) simulator. This craft, nicknamed "Hover-buggy", was a cruciform-shape hovering rig powered by two small jet engines oriented vertically *[see frontispiece]*, thus supported in flight by the downward thrust of the engines. Its purpose was to enable many different VTOL configurations, such as engines location and pilot position, to be evaluated on one rig. It somewhat resembled a giant bed frame.

Al White assigned Van Shepard as project pilot. Thus an early task for Van was to learn to fly a helicopter, as the flight controls of the Hoverbuggy would be similar to those of a chopper. He spent three weeks at helicopter flight school, and had ample opportunity to develop his proficiency as he participated in the final build and ground development of the Hoverbuggy. One thing Van did during his helicopter free-flight time was to pop in for lunch at his Mandeville Canyon home, landing in a nearby vacant lot!

Van took time out of his Hoverbuggy indoctrination to fly chase for XB-70A Air Vehicle #2's maiden flight on the morning of 17 July 1965. The script was just as #1's was, with White and Cotton aboard the Valkyrie at Palmdale, and Shepard and Fulton coming down from Edwards in the TB-58A chase. This time, though, there were no landing gear problems: AV #2 spent twenty-one minutes at super-sonic speed, achieving Mach 1.4, and landed at Edwards with few issues.

In August, it was time for Al White to relinquish the left seat to the other pilots. Cotton, Shepard, and Fulton each checked out in three successive flights of AV #2, with White aboard as copilot. For all its exotic character, Van did not find the Valkyrie a difficult plane to fly; its designers had done their homework well.

With two prototypes now flying, the XB-70A development pace was accelerating, as was the performance attained by the aircraft. On 14 October 1965, White and Cotton took #1 all the way to its design goals, at Mach 3.02 and 70,000 feet. On the ground at Edwards, there was much celebration by all members of the Valkyrie team. Even special "Mach 3" coveralls had been donned by ground crew members to greet AV #1 as it returned to its hanger. To this day, more than fifty years later, the Valkyrie remains the largest aircraft ever to attain Mach 3.

Back on the Hoverbuggy program, ground development was wrapped up by the end of October, and it was time for flight testing. As a precaution, there was a series of captive hovers, using a tele-scoping tether device attached beneath the center of the vehicle. Finally, Van Shepard piloted the maiden free-flight of the rig on 22 November 1965. What is ironic is that the first such vehicle of similar concept, built by Rolls Royce in the United Kingdom in 1954, was flown by a test pilot named R. T. Shepherd.

Van would fly most tests of the Hoverbuggy through early 1966. He was doubling up on his primary XB-70 assignment. On 6 January, he was pilot of AV #1 for another superlative of the Valkyrie program: he and copilot Fitz Fulton flew the longest mission by time, three hours, forty minutes, albeit entirely subsonically. During the flight the Valkyrie joined up with the aircraft it once was intended to replace, the venerable B-52. This particular example was the Air Force Flight Test Center's NB-52B, one of two carrier aircraft for the X-15 rocket plane and other air-launched research aircraft. The two bombers flew in formation at the end of the flight; it was notable that the immense Valkyrie was more than thirty feet longer than the Stratofortress.

Shortly thereafter Van received a call from one of his Van Dusen cousins, Marcella Nicholas. A journalism student at UCLA, she had heard about Van from family members, and wanted to submit an article about his career as a test pilot for a school periodical. They arranged to meet for a detailed interview; her article would indeed be published in the spring.

Late in January, the Valkyrie team received some accolades from state and local government at a dinner meeting in Lancaster. Both the California State Assembly and the Lancaster Chamber of Commerce took the occasion to recognize the accomplishments of NAA and the four pilots. There were speeches by government and Air Force officials. State Assemblyman Newton Russell gave the pilots framed resolutions that had been introduced at the state house in Sacramento, each lauding the individual's career accomplishments in aviation.

Sadly, in stark contrast to the euphoria surrounding Van's and the Valkyrie's successes, his marriage with Betty had now irretrievably broken down. The couple had agreed to separate; Betty was living at the Mandeville Canyon house with her sister Nancy, and Van was renting an apartment in Lancaster. A divorce would be final in the spring of 1966.

Fortunately for Van, this period was a busy one for him. The two XB-70A's were flying more than at any other time in the program; there were even days when both prototypes were flown. Van was aboard many of the flights, and often flew chase when he was not. Further, he remained involved with the Hoverbuggy flight program back in Los Angeles. It was easy for him to devote one hundred percent of his energy to his work at this otherwise difficult time.

Then, on Monday, 7 March 1966, came the flight which would

forever define Van Shepard's aviation career.

The day started routinely enough. With Van as pilot and Joe Cotton as copilot, Air Vehicle #1 took off from Edwards for its 37th flight, a two hour trip featuring air induction control and propulsion systems evaluations, plus stability & control tests. The schedule called for attainment of Mach 2.2 at 55,000 feet. It was Van's fourth consecutive flight in #1 as either pilot or copilot.

Shepard and Cotton had already flown together nine times in either the Valkyrie or the Hustler, and knew each other's flying style well. Climbing out of Edwards airspace, Van rolled the Valkyrie onto its course for the morning, a clockwise oval which would take it as far away as northern Utah. Chasing in the distance were the Hustler, with Al White at the controls, and, later, an F-104 Starfighter, with Fitz Fulton in the back seat. The first half of the flight went according to plan; the crew were completing all of their checklist tasks.

Suddenly, fate would intervene. The Valkyrie began to lose pressure in both of its utility hydraulics systems, which provide actuation power for everything other than flight control surfaces (which have their own dedicated systems). The big concern was that the "utilities" enabled gear deployment, an obvious need for landing the aircraft. The crew slowed to gear deployment speed, crossed their fingers, and commanded the gear to lower. After trying twice, they could only get partial deployment of the main gear. Most notably, the left side bogie beam was hung up in a vertical orientation.

Van Shepard was going to have to try to land the largest supersonic aircraft in US history on crippled gear.

PART IV

Destiny

Red Mountain, California, 7 March 1966, 9:46 am PST

The veteran pilots smoothly brought the giant bomber down its homeward flight path into Edwards. The chase planes continued to note that there was nothing visually untoward at all, except, of course, for the malpositioned landing gear. Cotton completed the fuel jettison without incident. Shepard was able to feel the difference afforded by the lighter weight; AV #1 was handling as nimbly as ever. The flight was cleared for a straight-in emergency landing on Rogers Dry Lake. Shepard executed a left turn, establishing a southerly heading toward lakebed Runway 17.

Edwards Data Control communicated the final plan. "Shep, we believe your best shot is to come on in with the gear just the way it is. We don't want to risk another cycling and not get as much as we've got right now."

Cotton and Shepard had already felt this way.

Shepard replied in his lyric Louisiana drawl, "Roger that, we agree. Piece of cake." He winked at Cotton; the briefest of smiles came to both. The ground team breathed a sigh of relief that they had full consensus.

The belief was that the weight of the Valkyrie touching down would force the right wheelset to finish swinging into the direction of travel. As for the left, given the entire wheelset was oriented vertically behind the centerline of the main strut, it was unlikely that the bogie beam carrying the wheels would ever level out. This "tiptoe" touchdown on the left side would cause the right wing to be lower than the left, but it was hoped that the right wingtip would still clear the ground at touchdown.

Shepard called, "Data Control, how 'bout a flare speed now?"

The ground replied, "Roger, Shep, we're going with 172."

172 knots was about 200 miles per hour; it was what Shepard was expecting. In a normal landing at that weight, they could probably have gone 10 knots lower, but the faster speed would enable them to reduce the angle of attack at flareout somewhat, providing critical ground clearance at the right wingtip.

The four program pilots, Shepard, Cotton, White, and Fulton, discussed what might be expected upon landing, bringing over eighty years of collective flying experience to bear on the challenge.

White suggested, "Shep, you oughtta smack the ground a little harder than normal; more load into the right gear might help it get closer to alignment."

But Fulton pointed out that care must be taken to prevent the right side wingtip from hitting the ground as the right gear touched down, given that the higher left side gear would result in about a five degree roll angle. Further, this roll angle would in itself be hazardous to control, as it would make the aircraft want to yaw to the right upon touchdown, which in turn could cause it to ground loop. While with luck not fatal to the pilots, this could cause the collapse at least one landing gear and damage the aircraft beyond economic repair.

Shepard himself hatched a plan to feed power to engine #6 (the farthest to the right) after touchdown, which might mitigate the yaw tendency due to the high left wing. All supported this bit of ingenuity.

Despite all this useful animated discussion, in the mind of each pilot was that this was Van Shepard's moment. All test pilots share a firm belief that the man in the left seat is to be trusted to use his own judgment and experience to do what is required to bring in a distressed aircraft.

In the distance loomed Edwards Air Force Base.

Shepard configured his flaps fully deployed, including the trailing edges of the canard surfaces not far behind the cabin. He and Cotton were busy setting, checking, and rechecking the position of every lever and switch for landing. They were constantly communicating with each other, and occasionally with the chase planes, the ground team, and the Edwards tower.

Shepard called out, "Tower, one last wind reading please."

"Uh, roger, Zero-Zero-One, we are two-seven-zero, still at zero-five knots. Max gust remains zero-niner. Kept it down for ya, Shep. Good luck."

Wind would not be a factor. Shepard thought, "Thank God for small favors."

The Great White Bird was flying beautifully, continuing to respond to Shepard's hand as if it read his mind.

"The calm before the storm," he thought.

On they sailed toward their destiny in the California desert.

Late in final approach, the Valkyrie was now over the lakebed. One of the chase planes began to call out its height above the deck.

"Sixty ... Lookin' good, Shep ... Fifty ..."

Retaining his sense of humor even in this moment of peril, Shepard muttered sarcastically to Cotton, "Is that right wheels or left?"

He held a knot or two above his flare speed, and mentally rehearsed his actions at flareout one more time. He had the Valkyrie aligned with the black reference lines demarking Runway 17. With their nose-up pitch attitude, he had to straighten himself slightly to see over the Bird's pointed snoot. He saw the red flashing lights of the emergency vehicles gathered to the west of his heading.

"This is it," he thought.

"Flaring now!!" Shepard called out emphatically, as he dropped the throttles and gave the yoke a nudge to the right to create a slight roll angle. Seconds that seemed like hours ticked by, as the aircraft sank. *Had he flared out too high given their reduced weight?* Suddenly 137 tons of hi-tech bomber impacted the lakebed, "tiptoed" left gear first. While balancing on one tire pair, he pushed the yoke forward gently to start to bring down the nose, which hopefully would create the needed right wingtip clearance aft. He allowed the aircraft to roll to the right toward the other gear, while adding a bit of left rudder. *Would that right wingtip hit?* Then the right gear impacted. Sure enough, the aircraft started to yaw to the right due to its roll attitude. He began to advance #6 thrust to counteract. Thank God, the giant delta was tracking well at this point, given it was banked right and still had its nose well into the air. *Coming down. Coming down. Would that nose gear ever touch?*

White called out from the Hustler, "Lookin' good, Shep, she's doing just what we wanted! Stay on that rudder!" But Shepard really didn't hear anything at that point; he was relying totally on his own instincts.

Finally the nose gear impacted. Immediately, the plane wanted to turn right even more. Shepard mashed the #6 throttle forward and added more left rudder. The 189 foot long aircraft now began to overreact, yawing back toward the left, even though it was banked right. This was the critical moment of the landing: he quickly took rudder out and pulled #6 back a bit, arresting the left yaw just short of catastrophe.

He worried about the left gear. *What if one of the overloaded tires blew? What if the wheelset suddenly flopped down from its tiptoe position, onto all fours? Could he react quickly enough?*

He continued to tune with the rudder and #6 throttle, but noticed that he wasn't dropping speed fast enough. 160 knots -- they were still careering down the course at over 180 mph! And no chutes, thrust reversers, or brakes! *Would he be the first pilot to use up Rogers Dry Lake?* He had to start reducing #6 thrust. Doing so, he could feel the Bird begin to decelerate, and added left rudder again, hoping to counteract the loss of the offset thrust.

At first he was holding nicely. In his ears, his buddies seemed ecstatic. Someone boomed, "Stay with it, Shep, you got it!"

But as he continued reducing thrust, AV #1 began drifting to the right, then more, then more. Though he was mashing his left foot down for all he was worth, he was losing rudder authority. He had no choice but to begin steering his nose wheel right, to match the path the plane was wanting to take. But, at least they were slowing.

Cotton called out, "No lights!", referring to the absence of fire warning lamps.

They kept turning farther and farther, but by now the plane had slowed enough that it could sustain the loadings imparted by the ever sharper right turn. The Starfighter zoomed back over-head, Fulton snapping photos from the back seat.

After what seemed like an eternity, XB-70A Air Vehicle #1 came to rest, in the middle of Rogers Dry Lake, California, miles from anything. There it sat on the dusty hardpan, six engines idling, still awkwardly tiptoed on its crippled left foot.

Gloved hands still firmly grasping the yoke, Shepard slowly exhaled. He turned to look at his copilot, who was looking back intently, his eyes telling all.

Joe Cotton matter-of-factly said, "Helluva Monday morning, Shep."

Outside, the Edwards first responders were racing to their aid. But with the Valkyrie's long rollout, it would take them minutes to get there.

No matter.

Van Shepard had just made the landing of his life.

*　　　　*　　　　*

SEVENTEEN
Mach 3!

The Tiptoeing Valkyrie. Van is third from right.

X B-70 PROGRAM FLIGHT 1-37 achieved the majority of its flight checklist, and serial no. 62-0001 landed safely despite failure of both utility hydraulics systems. It attained Mach 2.22 (1,450 miles per hour) at 57,000 feet, spending 62 minutes at supersonic speeds. Its 274,600 pound landing weight was the lightest of the program, and its 19,000 foot (3.6 mile) landing rollout the longest. The rollout took the shape of an upside-down letter "J", the plane turning 110 degrees and ending up more than half a mile to the right of lakebed Runway 17. Despite the dysfunction and damage sustained to its utility hydraulics and landing gear systems, Air Vehicle #1 returned to service just fifteen days later, with Joe Cotton and Van Shepard swapping seats as pilot and copilot.

On 19 March, flying as copilot with Al White in AV #2, Van hoped he would become the next pilot to go "triplesonic". But try as they might, the pilots could only coax Mach 2.93 out of the plane that day, despite reaching a program-maximum 74,000 feet altitude.

Van made nine more flights in the Valkyrie over the next five weeks. On one of them, as pilot in AV #2, he was cleared to go for Mach 3, but again fell just short, at Mach 2.95. In late April, he was excused from the program for four weeks, to focus on closing out the Hoverbuggy test operation, and then to take a needed vacation. While he was away, AV #1 was removed from service for two months of scheduled maintenance and upgrades, so the program was down to one aircraft. Upon his return, White then took a vacation of his own.

On Van's first day back, 22 May, he flew chase in the Hustler for Flight 2-40. On the agenda was participation in the 1966 Armed Forces Day show in progress at Edwards. America's two fastest bombers, the production B-58 and the experimental XB-70, along with a T-38 trainer, thrilled the crowd with two supersonic flyovers. It reminded Van of his days at Wright-Patt, only faster. While AV #2 roared by overhead with her chase planes, AV #1 was on the ramp below on static display. It made for quite a show.

Soon thereafter, the XB-70 program entered into a contract with a new government test program. At the time, the US government was providing funding for the design of a supersonic transport (SST) to enter commercial passenger service as early as 1974. The National Sonic Boom Program, or NSBP, intended to perform a long series of tests to thoroughly establish the sonic boom character of large super-sonic aircraft on the surface below, in order to fully understand the ramifications of the commercialization of such high speed transports. As the XB-70 was the only vehicle flying that was close to the configuration likely to be selected, and that could attain the speeds envisioned, it was contracted for the NSBP tests. After installation of specialized instrumentation, AV #2 was ready for the first test on 6 June 1966, the 22nd anniversary of D-Day.

Van Shepard and Joe Cotton would serve as pilot and copilot for this two hour Flight 2-45. It was the fifth consecutive flight of AV #2 with Van as pilot. In addition to the first set of sonic boom tests, XB-70A performance tests were also conducted. As part of the latter, Van climbed to 72,000 feet, trimmed out the Valkyrie for maximum speed, and advanced the six throttles to full afterburn. With his engines devouring a mile of stratosphere every 1.8 seconds, he watched his Mach meter creep past that magic number 3, to 3.05 – finally, after exceeding Mach 2.9 on no less than four prior flights! Joe Cotton, who had logged Mach 3 nine times now, feigned a yawn, taking a dig at his buddy. As it would turn out, 2-45 would be the last Mach 3 flight of the program.

Van landed, completed his post-rollout checklist items, taxied in, and pulled the Valkyrie into her hanger. He descended the stairs to a celebration with the XB-70 team, which, after flight debriefing, continued into the evening. The next day there was another celebration at L.A. Division headquarters, at which Van was presented a small trophy, featuring the number "3" fashioned out of the stainless steel honeycomb skin material of the Valkyrie.

When Van Shepard flew Flight 2-45, only about a dozen pilots had attained Mach 3 in an airbreathing vehicle. Even today, fewer than 400 have ever done so, most in the SR-71 Blackbirds. And this list no longer grows: there are no airworthy jets today capable of reaching such speeds. Put into perspective, many more people have orbited the earth in spacecraft; as of 2013, there were 533. The attainment of three times the speed of sound in an aircraft remains one of the rarest feats in the aerospace realm. After receiving his trophy, Van reflected back on the first man to do so, less than ten years earlier: his buddy Mel Apt, who ended up giving his life in the effort.

Meanwhile, there were changes in the wind for the XB-70 program. Their work essentially completed, NAA began to wind its pilots out of the program, which, along with the NSBP, would be transferred to NASA for further development. This transition meant folding in some new pilots for the Valkyrie. Al White and Van Shepard would be transitioned out over time, and replaced by NASA pilots. The USAF would still be involved, but would replace Joe Cotton with another pilot; Cotton would become XB-70 program manager for the USAF.

In the first moves toward this new staffing plan, the USAF had named Major Carl Cross to begin phasing in, to replace Cotton, and NASA had named its Chief Test Pilot Joe Walker to be its pilot in the program going forward. In the spring of 1966, both Cross and Walker had been attending XB-70 ground school and flying the Iron Cross simulator in Los Angeles, and were ready for checkout in the Valkyrie. The plan was for Cross to fly copilot in AV #2 with Fitz Fulton piloting, and then, two days later, Walker with Al White.

Wednesday, 8 June would be a busy day. In the morning, the Carl Cross checkout flight was scheduled, together with continued NSBP testing. In addition, a publicity photo session was arranged for the end of the flight, at the request of General Electric: five aircraft powered by GE engines, including the XB-70A, would be photographed while flying in formation. Due to a schedule conflict for Fulton, White was pulled into AV #2's pilot seat for this flight. Then, in the afternoon, Cotton and Shepard were to fly another set of NSBP tests in a second flight of the day for AV #2.

With nothing scheduled for himself until afternoon, Van arrived at Edwards later than usual, after AV #2 and its fellow photo subjects had taken off. He went to the NSBP office to review objectives for the afternoon sonic boom runs, and await the return of #2.

Suddenly, someone shouted that there had been a mid-air collision during the photo shoot. Pandemonium ensued, in which it was nearly impossible to tell just what had happened or who was involved.

Van rushed to the NAA office, where he knew that Test Operations head Zeke Hopkins would have been in continuous radio contact with the formation. Shaking his head, Hopkins told him that one of the formation planes, an F-104N with Joe Walker piloting, had collided with AV #2, causing the destruction of both. Only one ejection was observed among the three pilots involved; it was believed to be White. As information trickled in, it was ascertained that Walker and Cross had both perished, and that White had indeed ejected, but had sustained injuries upon his impact with the ground.

This was the darkest day of Van's aviation career to date. In the accident, he loses two more test pilot brothers, mere hours after celebrating his own attainment of Mach 3 in one of the aircraft now destroyed. Indeed, Van was the last man to land AV #2, two days earlier. He had known Joe Walker for fourteen years, and had just given him a tour of the Hoverbuggy in December. Although he had met Carl Cross only weeks before, he found him to be an engaging guy and another fellow Test Pilot School alumnus. And his boss Al White was now hospitalized.

What happened was that Walker's Starfighter had ventured too close to the Valkyrie as the formation tightened up, given the hazardous vortices surrounding the bomber's drooped wingtips. The Starfighter collided, was sent careering over the Valkyrie's back, shearing off most of the latter's verticals, and breaking in two, killing Walker. White and Cross did not even know they had been struck, due to the Valkyrie's immense size. The bird would continue flying straight and level for sixteen seconds before spinning out of control. Cross inexplicably could not eject, and went down with the aircraft. While White was able to eject, his escape capsule failed to deploy its impact cushion underneath, thus injuring him upon his landing.

The aftermath was ugly. President Johnson was briefed the same day, and ordered a full investigation. Fingers were pointed in every direction for weeks. Jobs were lost and reprimands issued, one of them unfairly delivered to Joe Cotton, as one of several individuals who, in theory, could have stopped the photo session. The US went from two flight-ready XB-70A's to zero in the space of a month, AV #1 already being down for maintenance and upgrade.

The Valkyrie team was in shock and rudderless for a while. No one knew what was going to happen with AV #1, NASA's plans, the NSBP, or anything else associated with the program. While it was not until after accident investigation concluded in August that plans could be made with any certainty, a team did, in the meantime, begin studying the potential to substitute AV #1 for #2 in the NSBP testing. While AV #1 was not quite as capable as #2, they concluded that this would be feasible, and began to plan for equipping #1 with the same sensing and recording equipment that #2 had. As soon as the go-ahead was given, the upfit of #1 for NSBP commenced, but it would be months before it was ready for flight.

This was a difficult time for Van Shepard. Not only was he grieving the loss of friends, he had also lost that ability to immerse himself in his work, a key defense against the depression associated with his recent divorce.

There were effects on the other pilots as well. Fitz Fulton decided to resign his Lieutenant Colonel's commission in the USAF, to become NASA's chief test pilot, backfilling the loss of Joe Walker. Al White recovered from his injuries soon enough, and was restored to flying status in September. But he had already been planning to wind out of the program, and never flew the Valkyrie again. He resigned NAA late in 1966 for a position as Manager of Research and Development with the airline TWA. Van's new boss at NAA would be Scott Crossfield, who was Technical Director, Research

Engineering and Test.

Its conversion for NSBP use completed, AV #1 resumed flying in November. The program would be supported by three pilots: given the loss of Cross and Walker, Cotton and Shepard agreed to stay on, along with Fulton in his new position with NASA. There were eleven flights of AV #1 through January 1967; Van was aboard seven of them. At this time, ownership of the XB-70 program was transferred to NASA. The aircraft was taken down for three months, for installation of additional instrumentation, and paint work including the application of NASA logos.

"Just another day at the office", winter 1966-67.

Early in 1967, things would change once again for Van, in a sense. North American Aviation merged with Rockwell-Standard, to form North American Rockwell Corporation (NAR). Ostensibly, there was no immediate effect at Los Angeles Division, but Van wondered what the change would mean for the longer term. Indeed, he would only be assigned to fly once more in the Valkyrie. His slot in the ongoing program went to a second NASA pilot, Don Mallick. Van's last ride was as copilot with Joe Cotton on 2 June 1967. He totaled 95.8 hours in the two XB-70's; this last flight, which attained Mach 1.4, would be the final supersonic flight of his career.

EIGHTEEN

TIFS

Total In-Flight Simulator, 1969

O N THE PERSONAL SIDE, Van was beginning to move beyond the pain of his divorce, as his involvement in the Valkyrie program wound down. He had returned to flying his own plane regularly, after neglecting it for much of his time with the XB-70 program; this indeed proved to be quite therapeutic. He decided to trade his old 1956 Cessna up to a newer 1963 172D Skyhawk model. He had begun dating as well, early on seeing a woman named Sandi. Later, he began dating Lois Marcum, with whom he would develop a long term relationship. And from Monroe, he received happy news of the arrival of his newest niece born to sister Frances. Named Bene, she would be the last of his fourteen nephews and nieces.

In September of 1967, Van was pleased to be able to help his cousin Norman "Mack Jr" McInnis celebrate a career milestone. Following receipt of his Navy pilot's wings in 1942, Mack Jr had gone on to a decorated naval career, with deployments as a carrier-based pilot in both World War II and Korea. Following that, he advanced into ship commands. Now a Captain, his career had reached its pinnacle with his appointment as Commanding Officer of the Essex-class carrier CVA-14 USS *Ticonderoga*. Prior to deployment to her fourth combat tour in the Vietnam theater, a ceremony was planned to formalize Mack Jr's installation as C.O., at Naval Air Station North Island near San Diego. He invited as special guests Van and Bill, his first cousins in the aerospace business. Bill could not attend, but Van did, and enjoyed the festive pomp of an on-board naval ceremony. It was good to reconnect with Mack Jr; Van was flattered to find that his cousin had been following his own career, and knew a great deal of his XB-70 accomplishments.

At North American Rockwell, however, the balance of 1967 was, for the most part, boring for Van. He was envious of his buddies Joe Cotton and Fitz Fulton: not only would they continue flying the Valkyrie, they also several times piloted the B-52 "motherplane" which carried the X-15 research aircraft to altitude for its drop-launches. Indeed, on 2 October 1967, Cotton flew the carry for the flight that achieved an almost unbelievable Mach 6.7, a record which still stands as the fastest manned aircraft flight ever. The X-15 pilot was Major William "Pete" Knight, who had flown chase for some of Van's XB-70 flights.

But with little in the way of new aircraft development programs in progress, Los Angeles Division simply did not have enough work to keep its own test pilots fully occupied. The ranks began to dwindle: among the most notable departures was that of Van's new boss, Scott Crossfield, to a position at Eastern Airlines. Van was often called into discussions in which pilot input was needed for decision making on future designs and concepts, but received few opportunities for test flying. NAR leadership had intimated that they were interested in him becoming chief test pilot for their Advanced Manned Strategic Aircraft program, which would later become the B-1 bomber. He was intrigued, but discounted the thought, as the program was many years from its maiden flight. Later they approached him again, this time with the idea of a non-flying leadership position. But the notion of flying a desk did not sit well with Van either. At one point he pondered a position with an airline, but he had never thought he could be happy in the commercial realm. Finally, word was getting around the aviation community that Van Shepard might be available for the right kind of test pilot job elsewhere.

One of those who approached him early on was Alvin "Tex" Johnston. He was one of the most famous test pilots of all, and had ended his longtime association with Boeing. Of late, he had been manager of Boeing's Atlantic Test Center in Florida, working mainly on space programs. He was most famous, or perhaps infamous depending on how one viewed it, for executing unauthorized barrel rolls with the Boeing 707 prototype in 1955, over a crowd of thousands at a boat race in Seattle. Spectacular as it was, it was a move which nearly got him fired. Earlier in his career, he was a competitor in the National Air Races, setting a race record in 1946, and he flew the XS-1 rocket plane early in its development. It is in the latter role that he and Van Shepard first met, at Muroc Army Airfield in 1947. Later, the men had gotten to know each other better, through both being Fellows in the Society of Experimental Test Pilots.

Johnston was in the process of setting up his own company, Tex Johnston Incorporated or TJI, to specialize in providing prototype build, development, and/or certification services to low volume aircraft manufacturers. He was targeting those companies creating new aircraft via heavy modification of production designs. Between

Christmas 1967 and New Year's Day 1968, he met Van over dinner in Los Angeles. He spoke enthusiastically about his plans, and invited Van to come to Goleta, California, a suburb of Santa Barbara, where he was planning to set up shop. TJI was going to share the facilities with Aero Spacelines Incorporated, or ASI, which was producing the Guppy series of outsize cargo aircraft by modifying Boeing 377 Stratocruisers. Johnston was also involved in the leadership of ASI, which in turn was a subsidiary of the holding company Unexcelled Incorporated.

TJI's first big contract was to fabricate a new type of trainer aircraft for Cornell Aeronautical Laboratory or CAL, of Buffalo, New York. The design called for modification of a Convair CV-440 twin-engine airliner to accommodate a reconfigurable second nose from a new aircraft design, forward and beneath the CV-440's cockpit. This would then enable pilot trainees to gain a feel in the air for how the new aircraft would fly. The concept, called Total In-Flight Simulator or TIFS, was that this would be far less expensive than building dedicated trainer prototypes of the new aircraft.

Early in January, Van toured the Goleta facility, located adjacent to the Santa Barbara municipal airport, and reviewed TJI's plans for the TIFS project and for the sharing of facilities with ASI. He then deep-dived with Johnston on exactly what the job would be. Johnston professed his admiration for what Van had accomplished over the years. He was drawn to Van's certification experience and rapport with the FAA, skills to be valued at TJI, and told him that his execution of the XB-70 "tiptoe landing" was an example of the kind of pilot expertise he was looking for. He offered Van the position of Vice President of Operations and Testing, reporting directly to himself. Van's compensation would be near double what he was receiving at NAR, with the potential for much more should the company grow as hoped. He did not take long in accepting Johnston's offer to start in February.

Van resigned from NAR, having worked there twelve and a half years. He thought it ironic that this was exactly the same duration as his active duty Air Force career. He was accorded a touching and celebratory going-away party one evening, in which Al White, late of TWA, joined. It was intimated to Van that Zeke Hopkins was also leaving NAR, to take a position with Douglas Aircraft. Such was the situation at NAR at the time.

Van reported for work at Goleta on 1 February 1968. Johnston charged him with everything related to getting the TJI operation up and running, from plumbing to human resources. Van immersed himself in his new job, often working fourteen hours or more a day. At the outset, there was little time for flying, but he did check out in the CV-440 which TJI had purchased to be the donor for the upcoming conversion to the TIFS configuration. The old airplane reminded him of his multi-engine days in the Army Air Forces, but what was new to him was the turboprop engines – his first exposure to this type of propulsion.

He grew weary of living out of a motel, but Goleta was too far from Lancaster to commute. Leveraging his newly augmented salary, he bought an oceanfront home in Santa Barbara at 151 La Jolla Drive. His relationship with Lois Marcum had become quite close; he tried to spend every Sunday with her. She was also fond of fly-

Van, Lois, and her three nephews

ing, and the couple would often go flying in the Cessna up and down the Pacific coast.

Van made multiple trips to CAL in Buffalo in the spring of 1968. During his return from one, in May, he arranged to visit his brother Bill at his home near Detroit, Michigan. Bill had been transferred there in 1963 by LTV Aerospace (formerly Vought), where he was now a defense programs engineering director. Van had not seen Bill in five years, nor his family for even longer; it was great to catch up as always.

One thing that CAL needed was a nose to graft onto the CV-440 for the TIFS build. They intended to use a Boeing 707, but were reluctant to spend the money to purchase an entire aircraft just for that purpose. Then, a solution practically fell into their lap. On 8 April 1968, a BOAC 707 loaded with 127 passengers and crew crash landed at London's Heathrow airport. Most of the passengers fortunately escaped. And, fortunately for CAL and TJI, while a good portion of the aircraft was destroyed, the nose section was largely intact! After negotiation with BOAC, TJI arranged to purchase the nose from salvage, and planned to ship it to Santa Barbara after British transportation safety personnel completed their investigations. Problem solved!

By midsummer, the TJI facility and staffing were beginning to look like a real enterprise. Van had hired a small staff of administrative, engineering, and technician employees, including Jim Shaw as a second test pilot. He had arranged for office space, hanger space, and a fabrication shop, mainly by negotiation with the facilities principal at ASI.

Tex Johnston knew that the work pace at TJI would become even more frenetic after the 707 nose arrived, and thus encouraged the team, including Van Shepard, to take vacations that summer. Van decided to take Lois to Puerto Rico in July, to fulfill two promises: one to Lois for a long getaway, and one to visit his Van Dusen cousin

THE TIPTOEING VALKYRIE

Betsy Nicholas Padín, an artist who lived near San Juan. Van and Lois had a wonderful stay with Betsy and her family at her residence/studio, and had fun touring the island afterward. During their return, Van had business at CAL in Buffalo, and Lois the same in Washington DC, after which they returned to California.

In the fall of 1968, the TJI team got to work cutting into the CV-440, preparing it to receive its "second nose". There was much to do; among the changes was shortening of the CV-440's forward fuselage, so that with the addition of the second nose the vehicle would not be too long. There was also a pair of verticals to add, one on each wing outboard of the engines: this was so that aerodynamic disturbances, such as crosswinds, could be simulated in the trainer cockpit. The idea was that the aircraft would be flown from the second nose by the trainees, with another pilot ready in the original CV-440 "safety cockpit" to take control should there be problems.

Van wistfully noticed in the media that XB-70A Air Vehicle #1's 83rd and last flight was on Tuesday, 4 February 1969, piloted by Fitz Fulton and Lieutenant Colonel Emil "Ted" Sturmthal, who had replaced Joe Cotton as the USAF pilot. They flew the aircraft from Edwards AFB to Wright-Patterson AFB, where they summarily signed it over to the Air Force Museum. How ironic that it would go on display right where Van spent so many formative years of his aviation career! He noted that not since his days at the Wright Air Development Center had he visited the museum; he would have to take Lois to see it someday.

TJI had hoped to have the 707 nose inventoried by the end of 1968, but it was not until April 1969 that it was released by the British. In order to expedite its shipment from the United Kingdom, an extraordinary plan was implemented. The TJI and ASI teams arranged to dispatch one of the Guppy cargo aircraft to Heathrow, to swallow the 707 nose in one piece, and to *fly* it to Santa Barbara! As well as saving much time for the TIFS build, the exercise provided great publicity for ASI and the Guppy program.

The grafting of the second nose to the TIFS fuselage took place immediately. Following that, there was structural work associated with the mated surfaces to accomplish, all of the mechanical and electrical connections to complete, and control strategies to implement. The aircraft was finally completed in the summer of 1969. Following paint work, a small rollout celebration was held on the ramp at Goleta. Taxi tests ensued, and then the newly configured, double-cockpit #N21466 took off on its maiden flight, with Van Shepard as pilot and Jim Shaw as copilot. For all his test pilot experience, it was the first maiden flight Van had ever commanded, apart from that of the Hoverbuggy. A rigorous test program followed over the next few weeks, with Shepard and Shaw splitting pilot and copilot duties. Tex Johnston even flew a few of the tests, after promising to perform no barrel rolls.

After validating the plane's basic airworthiness from the safety cockpit, it was time to assess the ability to fly the TIFS from the 707 trainer cockpit. Van moved down to the second nose, with Shaw remaining in the safety cockpit, for a series of exercises proving that the aircraft could be safely flown via the 707-based controls. The detailed setup and tuning of the controls to emulate actual 707 flight character were CAL's responsibility, to be done later in New York.

Finally, two days after Van celebrated his 45th birthday, he and Shaw took off in the TIFS to deliver it to their customer. Not wanting to push their new baby too hard, they would take two days to make the ten hour trip from Santa Barbara to Buffalo. Their route took them over the Grand Canyon, something Van had done many times in the Valkyrie. He found the view more enjoyable at 19,000 feet and 250 miles per hour than at 60,000 feet and Mach 2.5! They made the handoff to Cornell Aeronautical Laboratory on 7 October 1969.

NINETEEN

Guppies

Mini Guppy Turbine, 1970

W HILE VAN WAS BUSY with the build and testing of the TIFS aircraft, organizational changes were underway at Tex Johnston Incorporated. Aero Spacelines Incorporated had been receiving expressions of interest from potential customers for additional Guppy cargo carriers. To meet these needs, they had plans in place for new variants of the Guppy line, but did not have sufficient resources of their own to deliver. Given the completion of the TIFS project, it was natural that TJI resources be further consolidated with those of ASI. Tex Johnston had already been installed as board chairman of both companies, and had begun to implement this consolidation process. Van Shepard was transferred into a similar position, Vice President of Test Operations, of the combined operation, which would carry on under the ASI name.

Van went to work on the Guppies. He was already familiar with ASI's business plan, having attended meetings on the consolidation of operations for some time. His main assignment was to head flight testing of the firm's newest variant, the Mini Guppy Turbine, or MGT. The MGT was a repowered and more capacious version of the original Mini Guppy, or MG, which first flew in 1967 and was now in service flying contract cargo. The MGT would feature four Allison 501 turboprop engines, instead of the radial piston engines on the MG. These Allisons, very similar to those used on the TIFS, were harvested from retired Lockheed Electra airliners. The MGT's cargo hold would be a bit larger in most dimensions than the MG; it would be nose opening instead of tail opening, and, importantly, it would have the greatest load capacity of any Guppy to date. The modification of its donor Boeing 377 Stratocruiser was well underway as Van joined the program in late 1969. Among his first endeavors was to check out and log some time in the existing MG, between its contract job commitments.

In advance of what Van knew was going to be a busy first half of 1970, he planned a special vacation over New Year's with Lois. They were going to fly in the Cessna to Baja California, Mexico for a resort getaway. Then, on 30 December 1969, he received a call from his college-student nephew Bill Jr. *[the author]*, who had arrived in Los Angeles to attend the Rose Bowl football game; his school, the University of Michigan, was to play Southern Cal on New Year's Day. Coincidentally, Bill was staying at the International Airport Hotel, adjacent to the North American Rockwell plant where Van used to work. Bill was hoping to connect with Van during his stay, and have him meet his girlfriend (and future wife) Linda, who also made the trip. Van hated that he had to turn him down, as he and Lois were leaving for Mexico early on New Year's Eve.

Van followed the remaining MGT build activity closely. He came into the project early enough that he was being consulted for many flying-related decisions. This was an impressive aircraft: it was characterized by a giant cargo section that was uniform front-to-rear, unlike its predecessors, which had an ungainly tapering front-to-rear (hence the "Guppy" name). In February, this fourth Aero Spacelines model, Mini Guppy Turbine #N111AS, was rolled out to meet the public, on the same spot that the TIFS aircraft had the year before. Thereafter, ground development was able to proceed quickly compared to prior Guppy programs: as this build was quite similar to the original Mini Guppy, it was able to carry over certification of several already validated systems.

It was during this period that the Shepard family was undergoing a sad and difficult challenge. Van's father, Huber F. Shepard, was becoming debilitated by what is now known as Alzheimer's Disease. Signs of it had first been noticed several years earlier. Now 77, he continued to live at home with Marie, but this had become problematic for her: there were even episodes in which she had to fend off physical abuse.

Van and his siblings had recognized the gravity of the situation for some time. They felt powerless to do much about it, as is so often the case for the children of the afflicted. For Van, distance and the time requirements of his job, of course, did not help. One thing he decided to do was to give his mother a bit of a break: as a special birthday gift, he flew her out to California for a few days, to witness his maiden flight of the Mini Guppy Turbine.

Last known photo of Van, by Marie

Accompanied by Tex Johnston, Marie proudly watched from the tarmac as her son taxied out the giant cargo airplane, and took it into the skies for the first time. It was 13 March 1970, the day before her 75th birthday. It was an unforgettable experience, the first time she had ever witnessed Van take off in an aircraft other than his own.

As for all commercial aircraft, the MGT was to have its airworthiness demonstrated to the FAA via an extensive flight test program. Over the next few months, all manner of takeoff, landing, and cruise performance validation was to be conducted by Van and his team. He shared pilot duties with Harold "Hal" Hansen, ASI's chief test pilot.

On Tuesday, 12 May 1970, the MGT was scheduled for its twelfth flight, a series of tests at Edwards AFB to validate takeoff performance on three of four engines. Crew assignments were: Van Shepard, pilot, Hal Hansen, copilot, Travis Hodges, flight engineer, and Warren Walker, observer. Van had logged thirty-three hours in the MGT in its first eleven flights. The exercise consisted of a series of ten minute flights; for each, one engine would be shut down at or just prior to rotation, that critical moment when the nosewheel is lifted off the runway by the pilot. The aircraft must be able to safely complete the takeoff on the three remaining engines, and return for landing on the same runway.

THE TIPTOEING VALKYRIE

The day started early: the first takeoff of the MGT was at sunrise. All takeoffs and landings were on Edwards Runway 22, which Van Shepard had used innumerable times in his career. The first takeoff was a baseline run, with all four engines operating. For this and all subsequent runs, a full complement of flight data was recorded under the supervision of flight engineer Travis Hodges. Beginning with the second run, Van would have his copilot Hal Hansen shut down a different engine each time, and continue with his takeoff, using his controls to manage the changes in aircraft motion imparted by the "failed" engine. It is an exercise he had completed many times in his career. Four such shutdown takeoffs and landings were executed in succession without incident.

The next takeoff, a repeat of the shutdown of engine #1 (the leftmost), took place at 7:19 am. Three seconds after the shutdown of #1, Van rotated the nose up, and moments later the main wheels left the runway. As the plane started to climb, all appeared normal. Then, suddenly, it yawed and rolled to the left, losing altitude as it did so. Seconds later the left wingtip contacted the ground, which put the plane into a cartwheeling motion, in turn ramming the nose into the ground just to the left of the runway. The flight deck was destroyed in the impact, and a fire was ignited in the wreckage. Losing their lives in the accident were Harold Hansen, 44, Travis Hodges, 44, Van Shepard, 45, and Warren Walker, 43. They likely died instantly as the nose of the aircraft impacted.

The National Transportation Safety Board (NTSB) did a full investigation of the accident, as it does for all non-military aircraft incidents involving loss of life. There has been much speculation about the possibility of a failed component in the rudder actuation system, which could have caused the type of control loss experienced in the accident. Nonetheless, NTSB report #3-4387 concludes "Cause Undetermined". Van's flying career totaled 6,827 hours.

TWENTY

The Twin-Trunk Pine

N EWS OF THE ACCIDENT trickled out to Van's family, friends, and associates as the day wore on. Plans were made for a memorial service in Santa Barbara for all four of the crew members, to take place on Thursday, 14 May. Among those flying in for this service were Van's mother Marie and his siblings Bill and Sam Shepard and Frances Heidenreich. Also attending from nearby were Van's cousin Lois Skarda and sons, Van's girlfriend Lois

Marcum with members of her family, and some from the Oberg family. Of course, there were many from the aviation community in southern California.

The next day, the Shepard family members traveled to Monroe, Louisiana with Van's body. That evening there was a visitation at the local funeral home. Many other family members had come to Monroe, from Arkansas, Mississippi, and elsewhere, including Bill's wife Lois Shepard, who had helped care for her father-in-law H. F. while the others were in California. Sadly, it was noted during the visitation that H. F. did not seem to comprehend that he had lost his son.

The funeral was scheduled for Saturday the 16th. When Bill and Lois noticed that their children were the only nephews and niece of Van not present, they hastily made arrangements to fly them in from Michigan on Friday evening. However, a flight cancellation would prevent them from making it.

The funeral service took place at the chapel of Mulhearn Memorial Park cemetery. This was just a few miles east of the old store, which, although now owned by longtime employee Parker McGee, still operated under the name Shepard's. McGee himself was among the pallbearers. Attending both the Santa Barbara memorial and the Monroe funeral was Al White, who had as much to do with Van's career development as anyone. The mourners then assembled at the family grave site at the foot of a majestic twin-trunked pine. As Van's body was laid to rest, a coincidental, but fitting, tribute occurred: a Delta Airlines flight had just departed from nearby Monroe Regional Airport on Runway 04, one of the original runways of Selman Army Airfield. In climbing out, the DC-9 jet roared directly overhead, as if on cue. The significance was overwhelming for those in attendance.

Van's mother Marie later arranged for a beautiful full-length granite monument to adorn his grave. It sums up his life in several ways. At the monument's head, he is noted as being a "Captain U. S.

Air Force," and an "Engineering Test Pilot," including the symbol "X" from the Society of Experimental Test Pilots logo. In the middle of the monument is a stunning engraving of the XB-70A aircraft in flight, and at the foot is the inscription "He has at last become free, safe, and immortal, and ranges joyous through the boundless heavens."

Van Shepard's life is a perfect example of what one can achieve by identifying his or her passion at an early age, feeding it continuously into adulthood, and staying with it through the inevitable temptations to abandon it. He was not born into privilege or entitlement; he achieved what he did through passion and hard work. There were many points in his career at which he had to ante up and invest even more time and effort to sustain his dream; a less committed individual might have chosen to forsake what they were doing and take the lesser path.

At the same time, those he left behind would never forget how committed he was to his family throughout his career, even when he was burdened by the pressures of his job. Throughout this life of excitement that he led, of having acquaintances in high places, and of receiving accolades, Van never lost sight of the importance of family. Wherever he was working, which often seemed to be far away, he would seize every practical opportunity to reconnect with his family.

While Van's loved ones were distraught with his passing, they would feel that there was a certain inevitability to it. There could be no disputing that his chosen profession was a dangerous one; he himself had attended many funerals of associates who died testing aircraft, and knew of countless others. But he would persevere, doing what he was clearly born to do, and making our society and our country the better for it today.

Epilogue

V AN'S FATHER H. F. SHEPARD continued in his inexorable decline to Alzheimer's Disease. Though he did not appear to understand his son's passing, his symptoms seemed to accelerate in the months thereafter. When it reached the point when Marie was unable to care for him at home, he was moved into assisted living nearby. He passed away on 7 November 1974, just short of his 82nd birthday.

For years after Van's death, his legacy was sustained only by the memories and stories shared by loved ones he left behind. There was little in the way of tangible memorials, other than his beautiful grave monument. This began to change in 1976.

The Smithsonian Institution in Washington, DC had built its splendid new facility on the National Mall to house its extensive aerospace artifacts collection, the National Air and Space Museum. Opening in time for America's bicentennial, it would become the most visited museum in the capital.

Bill and Lois Shepard took their daughter Amy to see the sights in Washington in the bicentennial year. On their itinerary was a visit to the brand new Air and Space Museum. During their tour, they chanced upon a special display honoring fallen American test pilots. Sure enough, the names Harold Hansen, Travis Hodges, Warren Walker, and Van Shepard were on it, alongside the date 12 May 1970. It was an emotional moment; the family had not known of its existence. Bill later made arrangements to fly Marie to DC to see this memorial, which has since been removed.

Marie enjoyed good health into her later years. She was sustained by her faith, her lifelong gardening passion, and decorating her 1920s home on the Bayou DeSiard in Monroe. She died on Valentine's Day 1994, thirteen months short of one hundred years of age.

Van's life had a profound effect on that of his youngest nephew, Mark Shepard, his brother Sam's youngest child. Mark also took great interest in aviation, just as his father and uncle had, receiving his private pilot's license while a college student in northern California. In the summer of 1994, he attended a reception at an aviation art gallery in southern California, at which he met Fitz Fulton, who had flown with Van Shepard eighteen times in the XB-70. Fulton was pleased to meet this nephew of his late associate; the two spent much time in discussion about Van and the XB-70 program.

Just days after his return home, Mark received an invitation from the Commander of the Air Force Flight Test Center at Edwards AFB to attend a September 1994 luncheon marking the thirtieth anniversary of the first flight of the Valkyrie. Fulton had requested that Mark be invited. With great enthusiasm, he accepted, and returned to southern California for the event. He describes it as a wonderful affair with a "family feel" to it. He reconnected with Fulton, and was honored to meet the other surviving XB-70 pilots as well. They, in turn, were all pleased to have this close relative of their departed comrade representing him. As Mark met Joe Cotton, who lived near him in northern California, he established a friendship that would be sustained for years; he later came to know Joe's entire family.

His attendance at the luncheon was not the only highlight of the weekend for Mark. During his stay in Lancaster, he met Kerri Vermeer, of nearby Palmdale, in his hotel's lounge. The two enjoyed each other so much that they committed to stay in touch, and ended up marrying eighteen months later!

Van's ex-wife Betty married her neighbor Dave Maytag, who also had divorced, in the 1970s. Both continued to practice their affinity for flying, enjoying frequent trips to places near and far in Dave's Jet Commander. Betty passed away at 83 in 2015.

Meanwhile, XB-70A Air Vehicle #1 had become one of the most popular artifacts at what is now called the National Museum of the US Air Force (NMUSAF) at Wright-Patterson AFB near Dayton, Ohio. The aircraft had been moved (over seven miles of public roads!) with the rest of the collection to the museum's newly built facility in 1970. At the outset, there was not room for it indoors due to its size. For eighteen years, it was displayed outdoors in front of the museum, standing in the middle of what was formerly Wright Field's Runway 04/22. Ironically, that very runway was used many times by Van Shepard during his days at Wright-Patt.

In 1987, the museum was visited by Wendy Shepard Parlman, one of Van's nieces, and her husband Brian. While taking in the spectacle of the Valkyrie, they proudly noticed Van's name on the list of seven pilots stenciled on the air intakes. However, his surname was misspelled, with two p's. They called the error, which had occurred during a recent repainting, to the museum's attention, and it was promptly corrected.

Later in 1987, the Valkyrie was moved about a mile away to the museum's shops, where it underwent light restoration and maintenance while standing outdoors. It was unfortunately during this time that the author and his family made their first visit to the museum attempting to see the XB-70. They had to be content with seeing it at a distance; it would be years before they returned for close inspection. The plane returned to the museum as a featured exhibit in what was called the Modern Flight Gallery, to be housed indoors in perpetuity. Later, in 1996, the museum named its remodeled main restaurant "The Valkyrie Cafe". The dining room features a beautiful thirty foot long mural of the XB-70 in flight, etched glass booth dividers with a detailed side view of the plane, and even cafeteria trays emblazoned with a line drawing of the Great White Bird!

Back in California, the city of Lancaster is the closest sizable community to Edwards AFB, and is also near two other major aerospace facilities, the China Lake Naval Air Weapons Station, and US Air Force Plant 42, where the two XB-70 prototypes were assembled. In order to commemorate the contribution of pilots to aviation and space mobility, the city established its Aerospace Walk of Honor in 1990, lauding these pilots in a series of monuments placed along a downtown boulevard. Of the four original XB-70 program pilots, only Van Shepard had not been enshrined. Noting that his qualifications would align well with those of other honorees, the author began making plans to nominate him in 2014, only to discover that the program had closed to new honorees at the end of 2009.

Fortunately, there have been other opportunities to recognize Van's aviation accomplishments, at long last. The NMUSAF has a Wall of Honor of its own, along the exterior wall of its first building, which visitors pass by on their walk to the main entrance. A memorial plaque, in the form of an aircraft data plate, was arranged for, and installed as #791 in 2015. Also memorialized, after his passing in 2016 at the age of 94, is Van's buddy Joe Cotton, with plaque #1021. The week before every Memorial Day, there is a public ceremony at the Wall to celebrate the lives and contributions of all honorees.

Also in 2016, the NMUSAF opened a new fourth building for its expanding collection. Within it is the new home of its Research and Development Gallery, whose centerpiece is XB-70 #62-0001, the world's only surviving Valkyrie. As of this publishing, AV #1 remains the longest of the more than three hundred aircraft on display in the museum. For the June grand opening of the new building, the Shepard clan gathered for a family reunion and to celebrate Van's life. By serendipity, that week was also the fiftieth anniversary of his 1966 Mach 3 flight. Nineteen family members attended, from nine states, including both of his brothers. They shared stories and marveled at his mounts: an example of every Air Force plane he ever

flew is on display in the museum. Besides the Valkyrie, there is one other example in the collection in which Van flew the actual aircraft on display, the North Korean MiG-15 #2057, which he tested in 1954 right there at Wright-Patt. The collection also features the only remaining Total In-Flight Simulator ("TIFS") aircraft, this one the USAF "military" variant that followed the first "civil" plane which Van flew.

In other museums, there are two other airplanes which Van actually flew; both are in west coast collections. One is the only survivor of the 1940s Northrop flying wings, this one the N-9M "Little Wing" that Van flew in 1947 at Muroc. After decades in storage, it was restored by the Planes of Fame Museum in Chino, California between 1981 and 1994. Amazingly, the more than seventy year old plane is airworthy, flying in multiple shows yearly. The other is the Aero Spacelines "Mini Guppy" (the piston-powered version), flown by Van in 1969-70. This plane remained in service carrying contract cargo until 1995, when it was retired to the Tillamook Air Museum near Tillamook, Oregon, where it is open for touring today.

In 2017, one other memorial to Van Shepard's life was established, perhaps the most meaningful of all. This one is located in Monroe, Louisiana, a little over a mile from the site of his boyhood home. Since 2000, the Chennault Aviation and Military Museum has operated on the grounds of the old Selman Army Airfield. Named for Louisiana native General Claire Chennault of World War II "Flying Tigers" fame, the museum occupies one of the few remaining buildings that served Selman's navigator students during the war.

Upon visiting the museum, Sam Shepard noted that several hometown servicemen were honored in the collection, and inquired with museum officials as to whether there was interest in creating a display on his brother. Hearing the history on one of Monroe's favorite sons for the first time, the museum endorsed the idea, and plans were made for a display in its research and space section. A diverse collection of artifacts and photographs was rounded up from family members, and assembled into an attractive display by the museum staff. It was opened on 2 September 2017, with thirty-three family members attending. Van's siblings Sam Shepard and Frances Heidenreich did the reveal, which featured local television coverage.

Van Shepard had come home.

Appendix A

Milestones of Van Shepard's Aviation Career

c.1940 First airplane flight, Piper Cub, Selman Field, Monroe, Louisiana

1943 Enlisted US Army Air Forces, Shreveport, Louisiana

1944 Solo flight, Vultee BT-13 Valiant, Garden City Army Airfield, Kansas

1944 Graduated AAF Pilot School Class 44-I, received Instrument Rating, and promoted to 2nd Lieutenant, Pampa Army Airfield, Texas

1946 Jet aircraft piloted, Bell P-59B Airacomet, Muroc Army Airfield, California

1947 "Flying wing" aircraft piloted, Northrop N-9M, Muroc Army Airfield, California

1948 Promoted to 1st Lieutenant, Naha Air Base, Okinawa, Japan

1951 Graduated with Engineering Sciences degree, US Air Force Institute of Technology, Wright-Patterson AFB, Ohio

1951 Promoted to Captain, Wright-Patterson AFB, Ohio

1952 Graduated USAF Experimental Flight Test Pilot School Class 52-A, Edwards AFB, California

1952 Pilot, first demonstration of boom-type midair refueling of a fighter, Republic F-84G Thunderjet, Wright-Patterson AFB, Ohio

1953 Received Senior Pilot's Wings, Wright-Patterson AFB, Ohio

1954 Ejection from disabled aircraft, Republic F-84G Thunderjet, near Wright-Patterson AFB, Ohio

1954   Mach 1 flight, North American F-86D Sabre, Wright-Patterson AFB, Ohio

1955   First pilot to perform dead-stick landing of -C model of North American F-100 Super Sabre, Wright-Patterson AFB, Ohio

1955   Delta wing aircraft piloted, Convair YF-102A Delta Dagger, Wright-Patterson AFB, Ohio

1955   Honorable discharge, US Air Force active duty; hired as engineering test pilot by North American Aviation L.A. Division, Los Angeles, California

1959   Mach 2 flight, North American A3J-1 Vigilante, Edwards AFB, California

1964   Elected Fellow, Society of Experimental Test Pilots, Lancaster, California

1965   Copilot, first ever takeoff weight over 500,000 lbs, North American XB-70A Valkyrie, Edwards AFB, California

1966   Pilot, longest program flight by time, 3h40m, North American XB-70A Valkyrie, Edwards AFB, California

1966   Pilot, "Tiptoe Landing" on malfunctioning gear, North American XB-70A Valkyrie, Edwards AFB, California

1966   Copilot, highest altitude program flight, 74,000 feet, North American XB-70A Valkyrie, Edwards AFB, California

1966   Mach 3 flight, North American XB-70A Valkyrie, Edwards AFB, California

1969   Pilot, maiden flight, Cornell Aero Lab Total In-Flight Simulator, Santa Barbara Municipal Airport, California

1970   Pilot, maiden flight, Aero Spacelines Mini Guppy Turbine, Santa Barbara Municipal Airport, California

Appendix B

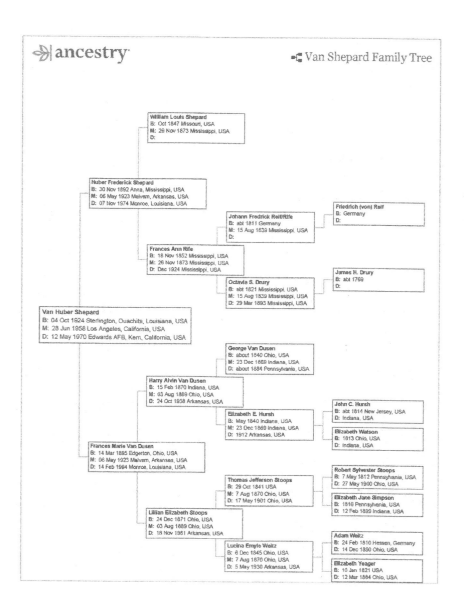

Appendix C

Partial list of aircraft flown professionally by Van Shepard

Aircraft	Date First Flown
Fairchild PT-19 Cornell	1944
Vultee BT-13 Valiant (first solo)	1944
Cessna AT-17 Bobcat	1944
North American B-25 Mitchell	1944
Martin B-26 Marauder	1944
North American AT-6 Texan	1945
Consolidated B-24 Liberator	1945
Beechcraft UC-45 Expeditor	1946
Douglas C-47 Skytrain	1946
Bell P-59 Airacomet (first jet)	1946
Lockheed P-80 Shooting Star	1947
Northrop N-9M Flying Wing*	1947
Douglas A-26 Invader	1947
Curtiss C-46 Commando	1947
Republic F-84 Thunderjet (straight wing)	1949
North American T-28 Trojan	1952
North American F-86 Sabre	1952
Lockheed F-94C Starfire	1953
Republic F-84F Thunderstreak (swept wing)	1954
North American F-100 Super Sabre	1954
Mikoyan-Gurovich MiG-15*	1954
Convair YF-102A Delta Dagger	1955
North American A3J Vigilante	1959

* actual airplane flown by Van Shepard on display in museum

Aircraft	Date First Flown
North American T-39 Sabreliner	1960
Convair B-58 Hustler	1962
North American XB-70 Valkyrie*	1965
North American "Hoverbuggy" VTOL simulator	1965
Convair CV-440 airliner	1968
Cornell Aero Lab Total In-Flight Simulator	1969
Aero Spacelines Mini Guppy*	1969

* actual airplane flown by Van Shepard on display in museum

This list contains only those aircraft that Van Shepard is known to have flown professionally. There are doubtless many others for which records do not exist; Van's flight log book remains unaccounted for.

Acknowledgments

I have many to thank in the preparation of this book, both for inspiring me to create it in the first place, and then for feeding me information used in writing it. As I said in the Foreword, Uncle Van has long been a hero of mine. However, I never really knew that much about his life, other than detail on his XB-70 flights available in the literature. I have my biggest hero, my father Bill Shepard, Sr., to thank for causing me to think about doing a biography. Back in 2011, he gave me a magazine article on his brother's aviation career, authored in 1966 by their cousin Marcella Nicholas, to whom I am also grateful. The article was an entertaining synopsis of Van's career up to that point, and it was then that I began to think about a book someday.

I am also grateful to my cousin Joe Skarda, Jr., whom I met at a 2013 family reunion at which we shared stories of our associations with Van. "Joey", who had worked at North American Rockwell after Van did, later sent me several back issues of the company weekly *Skywriter,* which prominently featured Van's activities on the XB-70 and "Hoverbuggy" programs.

I thank Van's brother Sam, sister Frances, and her husband Benny, for giving me several pieces of memorabilia about Van, including a cockpit voice recording from one of his early XB-70 flights. It was after hearing his voice for the first time in forty-five years that I began to covet "all things Uncle Van".

But it was a later event in Dayton where I was moved to become a writer. In 2016, the National Museum of the US Air Force opened a new fourth building to house their Research and Development Gallery, for which Van's XB-70 is a most impressive centerpiece. Three events associated with this opening moved me to undertake this effort. First, I was able to watch in October 2015 as the XB-70, the longest aircraft in the entire collection, was moved from its former annex site into the new building. Just seeing the Great White Bird in tow sent chills up my spine. Second, I was invited by the museum to write an article on Van's career for the Winter 2015-16 issue of their *Friends Journal*, which was great fun. And third, the Shepard clan got together for the fourth building Grand Opening on 11 June 2016. The highlight of the reunion came that evening, when the two brothers, Bill and Sam, took turns sharing many wonderful stories about growing up with their brother. It was then that I decided I had to write this book. Thus, I am again grateful to my Dad and my Uncle Sam, as well as to the NMUSAF, for their parts in helping sustain Van Shepard's legacy.

I have been assisted by other individuals who have provided priceless information and memorabilia. Diane Devins Etherson, a girlfriend of Van's from his Air Force days, gave me her recollections on their mostly long-distance relationship, including the photograph of them together. My second cousin Elizabeth "Bitsy" McInnis gave me information on her namesake grandmother, Van's Aunt Bessie, and her progeny, including Navy officer Norman McInnis. And I was fortunate to be able to learn a great deal about Van's ex-wife Betty Oberg Maytag through her sister Donna Oberg McMullin, who was, in turn, found by her cousin and a fellow genealogy enthusiast, Susan Bedal.

I must acknowledge my Senior English teacher, Marti Guthrie Sorgen. Was it mere coincidence that I ran into her again after forty-nine years, while writing this book? I think not.

Among the volumes in my personal aviation library, there are several from which I have drawn valuable reference information. These include Steve Ginter's *North American A-5A/RA-5C Vigilante*, Bill Holder's *Convair B-58 Hustler*, Graham Simons's *Valkyrie: The North American XB-70*, and no fewer than three works by Dennis Jenkins and Tony Landis, *Hypersonic: The Story of the North Amer-*

ican X-15, Valkyrie: North American's Mach 3 Superbomber, and *Experimental & Prototype U.S. Air Force Jet Fighters.* I also drew from Charles Eppley's Air Force Flight Test Center report *History of the USAF Experimental Flight Test Pilot School,* with its thorough description of Test Pilot School history at Edwards.

The ubiquitous online encyclopedia Wikipedia was also a valuable source for historical reference. It was helpful for interpolation to establish dates in which various flight test programs took place, and for providing biographical information on several of Van's associates in the aviation business.

Lastly, I have my wife and life partner Linda Ebert Ozzello Shepard to thank, for her proofreading of multiple drafts, but especially for putting up with my being chained to the desktop for the better part of a year.

Thanks again, everyone. It has been a wonderful ride.

Van's great-grand-niece Addison Shepard,
with her interpretation of The Tiptoeing Valkyrie

Index

Italicized page numbers refer to photographs

18th Airdrome Squadron, 79
25th Fighter Squadron, 81, 86
84th Fighter Squadron, 89
377 Stratocruiser, 182, 188
2750th Air Base Wing, 97, 103

A3J Vigilante, *131,* 133-137, 143
A-26 Invader, 70
Air Force Flight Test Center
    (AFFTC), 101, 126-128
Air Force Institute of Technology
    (AFIT), 67, 71, 87, 91-96, 100,
    127, 144
Allyson, June, 145
Ambrecht, John, 79
Apt, Mel, 127, 173
Arnold AFB, 150
AT-6 Texan, 54, 58, 64, 77, 80, 99,
    105
AT-17 Bobcat, 48
Atomic bomb, 56

B-24 Liberator, 55, 57
B-25 Mitchell, *47,* 50, 52, 74, 99
B-26 Marauder, 52, 54, 55, 151
B-47 Stratojet, 107

B-52 Stratofortress, 142, 161, 180
B-58 Hustler, 145-147, 172
"Bamboo Bomber", 48
Barksdale Army Airfield, 55
Bell, Beulah, 21, 22, 25, 26
Bell, Catherine, 21, 23, 25, 26
Blackburn, Al, 142, 144
BOAC 707 airliner crash, 184
BT-13 Valiant, 44, 45
Butler, Jimmy Joe, 101, 115

C-47 Skytrain, 65, 68
Carswell AFB, 146, 147
"Caterpillar Club", 110
Chennault Aviation and Military
    Museum, 202
Chennault, Claire, 35, 80, 202
Cimarron Field, 43
Civilian Pilot Training Program,
    (CPTP), 32-35
Clifton, Freda, 73, 82
College Training Detachments
    (CTD), 40, 41
Cornell Aeronautical Laboratory,
    182-186

Cotton, Joe, 13-15, 61, 121-123, 145, *149,* 150, 154-160, 163-180, 185, 198, 200
Crosby, Bing, *152*
Cross, Carl, 174-177
Crossfield, Scott, 119, 126, 132, 142, 176, 180
CV-440 airliner, 182-185

D-558-2 research aircraft, 119
D-Day, 46, 173
Dayton, Ohio, 11, 67, 91, 92, 96, 98, 104, 105, 116, 199
Devins, Diane, *107,* 118
Duchkar, John, 17, 18
Duchkar, Ruth Shepard, 17, 19, 26
Dugway Proving Ground, 131, 132

Edgerton, Ohio, 96
Edwards, Glen, 83
Eielson AFB, 115
Erwin, Nancy Oberg, *130,* 162

F-84F Thunderstreak, 111, 112
F-86 Sabre, 104, 107, 110, 111, 114
F-94 Starfire, 104, 105, 108
F-100 Super Sabre, *113,* 114-117, 126, 128, 131, 132, 135
F-102 Delta Dagger, 116
F-104 Starfighter, 61, 62, 163, 169, 175
Frost, Daisy Shepard, 27
Frost, Edward, 27

Fulton, Fitz, 62, 62, 101, 122, 145, *149,* 150, 154-163, 166, 169, 174-180, 185, 198

Garden City Army Airfield, 43-46, 48
General Electric Company, 92, 142, 146, 150, 174
"Gooney Bird", 65, 68

Hamilton Army Airfield, 73, 74, 77, 85, 87-91, 97
Hansen, Harold "Hal", 190, 191, 197
Hase, General F. W., transport vessel, 86, *87*
Heidenreich, Bene, 179
Heidenreich, Benny, 106, 114, 125, 129
Heidenreich, Effie, 134
Heidenreich, Fran, 127
Heidenreich, Frances Shepard, 26, 33, 73, 90, 91, 94, 105, 106, 114, 125, 129, 134, 145, 150, 179, 193
Heidenreich, Heidi, 150
Heidenreich, Lillian, 134
Heidenreich, Marretta, 105, 106
Heidenreich, Sonja, 145
Hodges, Travis, 190, 191, 197
Hondo Army Airfield, 57, 58, 64
Hopkins, Zeke, 100, 133, 143-145, 175, 183
"Hoverbuggy", *frontispiece,* 160-162, 172, 175, 186
Huff Daland Dusters, Inc., 24

Hughes, Howard, 155
Hutchinson, NAS, 118

International Date Line, 76, 86

Johnson, Lyndon, 151, 176
Johnston, Alvin "Tex", 181-184,
186-188, 190

Knight, William "Pete", 180
Konrad, John, 100

Langley Air Force Base, 84
Laughlin Army Airfield, 52-55, 57
Lear, Bill, 137
Liberal Army Airfield, 55-57
Lien, Wally, 66, 71

Mach 1 flight, Shepard's first, 111
Mach 2 flight, Shepard's first, 134
Mach 3 flight, Shepard's first, 173
Mallick, Don, 178
Malvern, Arkansas, 28, 30, 34, 41,
105
Mandeville Canyon, 138, 145, 150,
160, 162
Marcum, Lois, 179, *183,* 184, 185,
188, 189, 193
Maytag, Dave, 145, 198
McCollum, Fred, 25, 26, 43, 73
McCollum, Merlene, 25, 26, 43
McConnell AFB, 107, 118
McGee, Parker, 73, 194

McInnis, Bessie Shepard, 18, 19, 26,
30
McInnis, Norman, 30, 32, 33, 35, 180
Mid-air collision, XB-70A and
F-104N, 174-176
MiG-15, 107, 201
Mini Guppy, 188-189, 202
Mini Guppy Turbine, *187,* 188-191
Mississippi River 1927 flood, 20, 21
Monroe Natural Gas Field, 17, 21
Morton, General C. G., transport
vessel, 75, 76, 86
Mulhearn Memorial Park, 194

N-9M "Little Wing", 69, 83, 202
Natchez, Mississippi, 20, 27
National Advisory Committee for
Aeronautics (NACA), 84, 94, 100,
119, 126
National Aeronautics and Space
Administration (NASA), 84, 174,
176-178
National Air and Space Museum, 197
National Museum of the USAF, 92,
107, 151, 185, 199-201
National Sonic Boom Program
(NSBP), 172-174, 176, 177
Naval Air Development Center, 136,
137
Neville High School, 30, 33, 73, 84,
91, 94
Nicholas, Marcella, 162
Nixon, Richard, 132

No Kum-sok, 107

Northeast Junior College (U. of Louisiana - Monroe), 20, 32-36, 40, 53, 126, 152

North Island, NAS, 180

Northrop, "Jack", 70

O'Toole, Murray, 128, *130*, 136

P-51 Mustang, 66, 89, 126

P-59 Airacomet, 58, 64, 65, 203

P-80 Shooting Star, *63,* 64, 65, 68, 70, 71, 78-83, 85, 93, 94, 99, 104

P-84 Thunderjet, 65, 67, 68, *89,* 90-94, 104-110

Padín, Betsy Nicholas, 185

Pampa Army Airfield, 47-52

Parlman, Brian, 199

Parlman, Wendy Shepard, 145, 199

Pearl Harbor, 33, 45, 75

Piper Cub, 31, 40, 42

Planes of Fame Museum, 202

Point Mugu, NAS, 70, 120, 128

Popson, Ray, 101, 106

Port Columbus Airport, 116, 117, 133

Powell, Dick, 145, 150

PT-19 Cornell, 43, 44

Randolph Army Airfield, 54, 55

Roosevelt, Franklin, 32, 33

San Antonio Aviation Cadet Center, 41, 43

Selman Field, 30-35, 40, 51, 73, 194, 202

Severance, "Pappy", 31, 33

Shaw, Jim, 184-186

Shepard, Alan, 144

Shepard, Amy, 146, 197

Shepard, Becky, 27

Shepard, Betty Oberg, 9, *125,* 129, *130,* 132, 134-136, 138, 139, 144-151, 159, 162, 198, 199

Shepard, Bill, 20-22, *23,* 24-26, 53, 58, 66, 72, 73, 84, 87, 90-94, 119, 126-130, 146, 147, 150, 180, 184, 193, 194, 197

Shepard, Bill, Jr., 94, 128, 188, 189

Shepard, Claude, 26, 27

Shepard, Claude, Jr., 27

Shepard, Ella, 26, 27

Shepard, Greg, 118

Shepard, Huber, 17, *18,* 19-22, 25-27, 72, 90, 189, 194, 197

Shepard, Jean, 20, 134

Shepard, Jeff, 128, 147

Shepard, Julie, 129

Shepard, Kerri Vermeer, 198

Shepard, Linda Ebert Ozzello, 189

Shepard, Lois Stampley, 84, 94, 128-130, 147, 194, 197

Shepard, Mabel, 27

Shepard, Marie Van Dusen, *18,* 19, 22, 25-27, 72, 90, 98, 125, 130, 152, 189, 190, 193, 194, 197, 198

Shepard, Mark, 145, 198

Shepard, Peggy Walters, 106, 118, 129, 147
Shepard, Sam, 128, 147
Shepard, Samuel E., 25, 31, 73, 84, 90, 91, 94,106, 117, 118, 129, 145, 147, 193, 198, 202
Shepard, William Louis, 20
Shepherd, R. T., 161
Sherrouse School, 24, 105
Skarda, Joe, 129, 130
Skarda, Joe, Jr., 129
Skarda, Larry, 129
Skarda, Lois Van Dusen, 127, 129, 130, 193
Society of Experimental Test Pilots, (SETP), 127, 154, 181, 195
"Spruce Goose", 155
SR-71 Blackbird, 173
Sterlington, Louisiana, 18, 26, 30
Sturmthal, Emil "Ted", 185
Suffolk County AFB, 113

T-28 Trojan, 99
T-38 Talon, 154, 172
T-39 Sabreliner, 137, 138, *141,* 143, 144, 151
TB-58A Hustler, 16, 60, 61, 145-147, 154-158, 163, 168, 172
Ticonderoga, CVA-14 carrier, 180
Tillamook Air Museum, 202
Total In-Flight Simulator (TIFS) aircraft, *179,* 182-189, 201
Truman, Harry, 56

Typhoon Flora, 80
Typhoon Libby, 85, 86, 90

Unexcelled Incorporated, 182
USAF Experimental Flight Test Pilot School, 92, 95-101, 106, 119, 127, 133, 144, 145, 175

Valkyrie, name derivation of, 142
Van Dusen, Clyde, 30
Van Dusen, Clyde Erwin, 30, 34, 41
Van Dusen, Harry, 27, 28
Van Dusen, Lillie, 27, 28
Van Veneer Company, 26-28
V-E Day, 54
V-J Day, 56

Walker, Joe, 100, 174-177
Walker, Warren, 190, 191, 197
Weitz, Adam, 96
Weitz, Elizabeth, 96
White, Al, 15, 16, 60, 101, 119, 128, *130,* 132, 136, 142-147, *149,* 150, 154, 155, 158-161, 163, 166, 168, 172-176, 183, 194
Williams AFB, 100
Williams, Elizabeth, 19
Williams, Dr. J. B., 18
Woolman, C. E., 24
Wright Air Development Center (WADC), 95, 97, 100, 101, 104-108, 115, 116, 186
Wright Brothers, 92

Wright-Patterson AFB, 91-98, 103-
109, 114-117, 172, 185, 199, 201

X-1 (XS-1) research aircraft, 67, 68,
71, 78, 100, 181
X-2 research aircraft, 127
X-5 research aircraft, 101, 106

X-15 research aircraft, 119, 132, 141,
142, 161, 180
XB-35 "Flying Wing", 66

YB-49 "Flying Wing", 83
Yeager, Chuck, 78, 92

Printed in Great Britain
by Amazon